CAN DISTANCE LEARNING INCREASE STUDENTS NUMBER

JOHN LOK

Made with ♥ on the Notion Press Platform
www.notionpress.com

Contents

Preface

Introduction

Our business society had developed long time from farming period to manufacturing period, then to service industry period, till to nowadays technology service and manufacturing period. It brings this question: Can technology or human behavior may influence economic development? Human ourselves foolish or enjoyment behavior whether which can bring economic recession? If human can forgive to do enjoyment behavior, we can help economic growth? I shall apply behavioral economic theory to indicate cases to attempt to explain these questions.

In the beginning, I shall indicate my opinions to explain why computer and internet technology will be the best tool to solve any educational challenges as well as I shall recommend how any education organizations can apply this new technology to educate students effectively and efficiently.

In generaly, educators think that education means considerably more than just teaching a student to read, write and numbers only. However, nowadays, computers, the internet nd advanced electronic are becoming essential in everyday life and have changes the way information is gathered. So, it brings these questions such as, how is this new technology utilized and managed by teachers to solve any teaching challenges more easily? Will this new technology have an important role to play in widening the resource and knowledge base for all students? Can technology is applied to school to bring teacher education behavior to be improved? Can technology or distance learning education method help schools to raise student number? Can distance learning need increase?

Prologue

Contents

Chapter 1 Explaining supply and demand economic theory relationship between technological learning method and students number

The difference between past and nowadays economists their demand and supply economic theory explanation?

What are the relationship between demand and supply?

p.3-20

Chapter 2 Human social job change demand and supply relationship Why social behavior may influence organizational strategy needs to be changed p.21-51

Human Behavioral network job brings social
economic benefits

What does human network job mean

Why human network job behavior may influence economy

Robots take our jobs behavioral and economy influences

Robot job behavior brings economy influences

Chapter 3 Human intellectual demand and supply behavior relationship Intellectual human economic behaviors p.52 74

What does intellectual human economic behaviors
mean ?

The relationship between social change and human
behavior

Chapter 4
Technology or human behavior whether may influence economic growth or recession

Human Behavioral network job brings social
economic benefits

What does human network job mean

Why human network job behavior may influence economy

Explaining supply and demand economic theory relationship between technological learning method and students number

The difference between past and nowadays economists their demand and supply economic theory explanation?

The law of supply and demand defines the relationship between the price of a given good or product and the willingness of people to either buy or sell it. Generally, as the price of a good increases, people are willing to supply more and demand less. These economists had explained economic demand and supply theory as below:

Philosopher John Locke is credited with one of the earliest written descriptions of this economic principle in his 1691 publication, Some Considerations of the Consequences of the Lowering of Interest and the Raising of the Value of Money. Locke addressed the concept of supply and demand as part of a discussion about interest rates in 17th-century England. Many merchants wanted the government to lower the cap on interest rates charged by private lenders so that people could borrow more money and thus purchase more goods. Locke argued that the free-market economy should set rates because government regulation could have unintended consequences. If the lending industry were left alone, interest rates would regulate themselves, Locke wrote: "The price of any commodity rises or falls by the proportion of the number of buyers and sellers."

Sir James Steuart's Inquiry into the Principles of Political Economy, published in 1796, was the first known printed use of the term "supply and demand." When Steuart wrote his treatise on political economy, one of his main concerns was the impact of supply and demand on laborers.

Adam Smith dealt extensively with the topic in his 1776 epic economic work, The Wealth of Nations. Often referred to as the Father of Economics, Smith explained the concept of supply and demand as an "invisible hand" that naturally guides the economy. According to Smith, the invisible hand is the automatic pricing and distribution mechanisms in the economy. Smith described a society in which bakers and butchers provide products that individuals need and want, providing a supply that meets demand and developing an economy that benefits everyone. It is important to note that Smith's ideas haven't gone without critique over the years since his ideas were first published, though. Over time, his ideas have been added to in order to represent the changing times and include concepts such as marginal utility, comparative advantage, entrepreneurship, the time-preference theory of interest, and monetary theory.

One of Marshall's most important contributions to microeconomics was his introduction of the concept of price elasticity of demand, which examines how price changes affect demand. In theory, people buy less of a particular product if the price increases, but Marshall noted that in real life, this behavior was not always true. The prices of some goods can increase without reducing demand, which means their prices are inelastic. Inelastic goods tend to include items such as medication or food that consumers deem crucial to daily life. Marshall argued that supply and demand, costs of production, and price elasticity all work together.

Nowadays economists they explain demand and supply economic theory, they have some different to past economists whose explanation as below:

How Does Supply and Demand Work? The law of supply and demand is a theory that explains the interaction between the sellers of a resource and the buyers of that resource. Generally, as price increases, people are willing to supply more and demand less and vice versa when the price falls. What does the bottom line mean. Despite the origins of the law of supply and demand beginning hundreds of years ago, it's still a topic frequently referenced and utilized today in economic theory and discussions. The theory has developed over time to accommodate recent technological and economical advancements, but the basic ideas of the theory remain largely the same.

Does demand depend on supply?

Supply and Demand Determine the Price of Goods and Quantities Produced and Consumed. Consumers may exhaust the available supply of a good by purchasing a given good or service at a high volume. This leads to an increase in demand. As demand increases, the available supply also decreases.

What does market demand depend on?

Market factors affecting demand of consumer goods. The demand for a good increases or decreases depending on several factors. This includes the product's price, perceived quality, advertising spend, consumer income, consumer confidence, and changes in taste and fashion.

Who controls the demand in supply and demand?

Supply and demand are in turn determined by technology and the conditions under which people operate. At one extreme, the market could be populated by a large number of virtually identical sellers and buyers (for example, the market for ballpoint pens).

What are the two laws of demand and supply?

The law of demand holds that the demand level for a product or a resource will decline as its price rises, and rise as the price drops. Conversely, the law of supply says higher prices boost supply of an economic good while lower ones tend to diminish it.

What factors affect demand and supply?

Price fluctuations are a strong factor affecting supply and demand. When a product gets expensive enough that the average consumer no longer feels it is worth it to buy the product, then the demand declines. This leads to cuts in production that will hopefully stabilize the product's value.

What factors affect demand and demand?

Demand may be defined as the quantity of a commodity that a consumer is able and willing to buy, at each possible price, over a given period of time. • Essential elements of demand are quantity, ability, willingness, prices, and period of time.

Which factors affect supply?

Generally, the supply of a product depends on its price and other variables such as the cost of production.

    a. Price. Price can be understood as what the consumer is willing to pay to receive a good or service. ...

b. Cost of production. ...

c. Technology. ...

d. Governments' policies. ...

e. Transportation condition.

How does supply and demand work together?

It's a fundamental economic principle that when supply exceeds demand for a good or service, prices fall. When demand exceeds supply, prices tend to rise. There is an inverse relationship between the supply and prices of goods and services when demand is unchanged.

What happens to supply when demand increases?

An increase in demand, all other things unchanged, will cause the equilibrium price to rise; quantity supplied will increase. A decrease in demand will cause the equilibrium price to fall; quantity supplied will decrease.

What is the theory of demand?

Demand theory describes the way that changes in the quantity of a good or service demanded by consumers affects its price in the market, The theory states that the higher the price of a product is, all else equal, the less of it will be demanded, inferring a downward sloping demand curve.

What are the 4 basic laws of supply and demand?

1) If the supply increases and demand stays the same, the price will go down. 2) If the supply decreases and demand stays the same, the price will go up. 3) If the supply stays the same and demand increases, the price will go up. 4) If the supply stays the same and demand decreases, the price will go down.

The different types of demand are as follows:

i. Individual and Market Demand: ...

ii. Organization and Industry Demand: ...

iii. Autonomous and Derived Demand: ...

iv. Demand for Perishable and Durable Goods: ...

v. Short-term and Long-term Demand:

What creates demand for a product?

You can create demand for a unique product if you can manage to solve a persistent problem for the consumer. People are always running away from pain, and providing them with an outlet is a sure-fire way to create massive demand for your goods.

What are the 7 factors that affect supply?

The seven factors which affect the changes of supply are as follows: (i) Natural Conditions (ii) Technical Progress (iii) Change in Factor Prices (iv)

Transport Improvements (v) Calamities (vi) Monopolies (vii) Fiscal Policy.

What can affect demand?

Factors Affecting Demand

Price of the Product. ...

The Consumer's Income. ...

The Price of Related Goods. ...

The Tastes and Preferences of Consumers. ...

The Consumer's Expectations. ...

The Number of Consumers in the Market.

What are the three factors affecting demand?

The demand for a product will be influenced by several factors:

Price. Usually viewed as the most important factor that affects demand. ...

Income levels. ...

Consumer tastes and preferences. ...

Competition. ...

Fashions.

What are the 4 factors of supply?

The four factors that can shift the supply curve include natural conditions, input prices, technology, and government.

What causes increase in supply?

If the cost of production is lower, the profits available at a given price will increase, and producers will produce more. With more produced at every price, the supply curve will shift to the right, meaning an increase in supply.

What causes supply changes?

A change in supply is an economic term that describes when the suppliers of a given good or service alter production or output. A change in supply can occur as a result of new technologies, such as more efficient or less expensive production processes, or a change in the number of competitors in the market.

Is supply and demand a good strategy?

When it comes to profit placement, supply and demand zones can be a great tool as well. Always place your profit target ahead of a zone so that you don't risk giving back all your profits when the open interest in that zone is filled.

How is demand created?

Demand creation is a process that fuels the revenue pipeline so the sales team can meet or exceed their quotas. In other words, it takes your big idea

— the creative appeal of your brand — and turns it into sales. That sounds a lot like demand generation, which often gets confused with lead generation.

What are the two parts of demand?

Economists define demand as the quantity of a good or service that buyers are willing and able to buy at all possible prices during a certain time period. Notice that there are two components to demand: willingness to purchase and ability to pay.

Can we control demand?

If you're willing to think and act strategically, you can easily manipulate the laws of supply and demand. It should be surprising to learn, however, that by manipulating the laws of supply and demand, you can make more profit in less time and with far fewer headaches

How do you control demand?

Here are five short-term actions to improve your demand variability management plans in this time of uncertainty:

Maintain transparent, proactive relationships with your suppliers. ...

Activate alternate sources of supply. ...

Reduce lead times. ...

Update inventory policy and planning. ...

Align supply and demand management.

What are the 8 types of demand?

There are 8 states of demand: negative demand, no demand, latent demand, falling demand, irregular demand, full demand, overfull demand and unwholesome demand.

What is Demand?

Types of Determinants of Demand. Every factor has a unique impact on demand. ...

Price of the Product. ...

The Income of the Consumers. ...

Number of Buyers in the Market. ...

Consumer's Expectations. ...

Tastes and Preferences of The Consumers. ...

Complement Goods. ...

Substitute Product.

What is theory of supply?

The law of supply is a fundamental principle of economic theory which states that, keeping other factors constant, an increase in price results in an increase in quantity supplied. In other words, there is a direct relationship between price and quantity: quantities respond in the same direction as price changes.

What are the types of supply?

There are five types of supply—market supply, short-term supply, long-term supply, joint supply, and composite supply.

Which comes first supply or demand?

Demand comes first and it's followed by the corresponding supplies. Supply and demand are both very important to economic activity. Supply is the total amount of a particular good or service available at a given time to consumers at a given price. Demand is a representation of a consumer's desire to purchase goods and services; it acts as a measurement of a consumer's willingness to purchase a specific good or service at a given price. These two economic forces influence each other; they are both important for the economy because they impact the prices of consumer goods and services within an economy and the quantities produced and consumed. Supply and demand are both keys to understanding the economy because they reflect the prices and quantities of consumer goods and services within an economy.

What are the relationship between demand and supply?

According to market economy theory, the relationship between supply and demand balances out at a point in the future; this point is called the equilibrium price.

Economists and companies analyze the relationship between supply and demand when making strategic product decisions. Both economists and companies analyze the relationship between supply and demand when making strategic product decisions. The assumption behind a market economy is that supply and demand are the best determinants for an economy's growth and health.

Consumer Behavior Influences Demand

One way that companies or economists might analyze this relationship is to create graphs that chart the equilibrium price of certain goods and services in order to determine product development and their production schedule. Consumer behavior dictates which products are produced and sold because consumers create the demand that companies attempt to meet. As a result, companies may study consumer behavior in an attempt to understand the current demand and predict future demand. It is vital that companies maintain the capacity to produce enough of a good or service that they can satisfy consumer demands.

Supply and demand are two sides of the same market coin. Generally, supply is how much of something is available or will be produced at a certain price. Demand is how much of something people want to purchase or consume at a certain price. One way to develop a more precise relationship between the two is to consider how the price of something affects its supply and its demand. Generally when the price of a good goes up, so does the supply, since firms are willing to create more when they can sell at higher prices. But when the price of a good goes up consumers will, at the same time, generally demand less. It is the interaction of supply and demand that determines how much will be produced and consumed and at what price, converging to a state known as equilibrium.

Human social job change demand and supply relationship

Human Behavioral network job brings social economic benefits

Whether human social job change it depends on social job demand more or job supply more? What does human network job mean ? Why may human network job be popular? Why human network job behavior may influence economy ?

Nowadays internet is popular to use. We can apply internet to find data , search any new things, even earn money. Why does internet may become huma network job source. For example, e-publish may be one kind of new human network job. Any authors may apply internet channel to help them to sell electronic or paper books from e-publisher web store. They may apply facebook, you tub etc. any online channel to promote themselves new books to let new readers to know whether when they may buy themselves favourable new topic books to read from electronic publisher web store.

Thus, future electronic publisher industry may help any authors to build internet network platform to help them to sell and promote ot advertise their any one new electronic or paper book topic to let global any one reader to choose to buy their any new topic books from electronic publisher web store easily and conveniently. However, it implies that electronic network platform author may be one kind of future new human network job in our societies.

How electronic network platform author job may bring economy benefit in macro economy view? A person can have few friends, contacts and still be very influential if these few

friends and contacts are themselves highly influential, e.g. one author must not need to know any one reader in global society. When they like to choose any electronic books from electronic internet network platform. They may become the author's any one topic book buyer, when they feel the author's any one topic book is fun and attract they make decision to buth the strange author whose the topic book from electronic book publisher's platform web store conventiently in short time. Although, they are strangers, they do not know themselves , but the reader can understand what it way that made Google from writing platofrm to create new creative mind and typing network job method to replace traditional hand writing book method for global authors. It will be one kind of new human network writing job.

Hence, global any one reader can apply an innovative search engine , such as google.com to find whether whom author personal new topic books are value to read from internet.

Then, the electroniuc publisher's web store may be new book store platform sale network to help the author to sell many electronic or paper books from electronic network platform

in short time. So, internet may be future new network plaform to help global any one author to create network writing job absolutely. Furthermore, internet may be popular social media

to help any one author to build goold relationship between his/her readers. It is one kind of new network, human network job. New authors do not need to buy many paper books to prepare to put in any one book shop warehouse. Their every book can print on demand to reduce out of book stock in any one book shop. They may choose to sell either electronic books or paper books both from any one book publisher web store. So, electronic network platform may be one kind of good writing channel to help human authors to create income and it can also help authors to bring new creative mind and new topic fun content books to let readers to know and buy to read from electronic publisher network platform.

Why does human behavior may be one kind of new human network job to bring global economic advantages. ALthough, it may be free income or without inocme, but the person does the network behavior, his/her behavior may be bring advantages to influence many other people's health.

For this case, when a worker in a coffee shop in an airport gets a vaccination aganinst the flu, it does not only helps him or her stay healthy, but also helps the many travellers who might otherwise have been inflected if that workers caught the flu. So, the externality , the result implies the vaccination of even a part of a community conveys benefits to the whole community. For example, governments pay special attention to the vaccinations of school children, teachers, health mothers, and the elderly, categories of people particularly susceptible not only to catching, but also to transmitting a disease.

It is not accidential that governments are heavily involved with vaccination . When there are externalities, free market, fail to persuade individual incentives with society's

their the worker's decision of whether to get a vaccine ends up attracting whether other people get sick. The workers might not fully take all these other people's potential suffering into account when making her or his vaccination decision.

As Stanford University does many suggestions, understand this and tries to help them make the right decisions and so providers free flu vaccines for its staff and students.

Small pockets of unvaccinated individuals can allow a disease to gain a spread more widely well-being. For example, parent weighing the costs and benefits of a vaccine for their child is not always thinking of the consequences of that vaccination to other people. THese are markets in which subsidizing or regulating behavior can make everyone better off. Because the reason for requiring that a child be vaccinated before enrolling in school is not just to protect that child, because each child's vaccination affects others via potential contagions.

On conclusion, it seems that many traditional paper book publish business begain to change to electronic book publish business. Due, to online technology existence, it influences many readers choose to buy electronic books to read. Hence, due to readers reading demand change which is from paper book reading habit to electonic book reading habit.Then,it explains that electornic book supply number depends on electronic book reader reading demand in economic view.

Robots take our jobs behavioral and economy influences

Robot job behavior brings economy influences

Whether robot labor needs are depended on employer labor demand more or robot labor number supply more? If one day robots can replace human to do simple, even complex jobs. They will bring what influences to our global societial economy.The popular economic refrain declares that the global middle class is dying and robots will soon take our jobs, e.g. shopping center customer service jobs, library service jobs, cinema ticket sale jobs, restaurant kitchen cooker jobs,
even, bus drivers, taxi drivers etc. public transport driving jobs, accountant, doctors etc. professional jobs. Whether it is beautiful or petty matter if our future societies have many human jobs can be replaced to do from robots. Businessman must may reduce to employ employees and reduce to pay salary or wage, when robots can be replaced to do their employees tasks. But, societies must bring unemployement rate rises , due to societies will have many people loss jobs when their employers choose to buy robots to serve their clients or do any office tasks or customer service or cleaning etc. tasks.

In micro economy view, employers may save money in long term, but in macro economy view, it will cause unemployment ratio rises , even crime rate rises when there are many people lose jobs in societies. These models of doom, though, fail to account for the hundreds of businesses riding the waves of change in their industries when robots may be invented to replace human to do many simple , even complex tasks in our future societies.

WE may image that one small factory needs to manufacture fishes canes to sell to supermarket, the small , cheaper stuff and higher margin parts of the fishes manufacture industry. Before, this factory needs to employe many human factory workers need to help every fresh customer makeing the perfect fishing gear, designed for performance, durability, and cost in order to achieve to manufacture every fish cane in whole fished processing manufacturing stages. Every worker needs to spend about 15 to twenty minutes to finish every fish cane , till to delivery to any supermarket to sell. If this fish canes manufacturing factory can apply manufacturing robots to help them to finish any one working tasks , every robot can only spend five minutes to finish whole fresh fish cane manufacturing process. Thus, every robot can
help this factory save 10 to 15 minutes time to finsh every fish cane manufacturing process. IN fact, time is money, because when every robot can help this factory to reduce 10 to 15 minutes time to compare human

worker. Then, this factory can finish about 20 fish canes in one hour if it can use robot to help it to manufacture fish canes. Otherwise, if this factory still use human workers to help it to manufacture fish canes, then it can finsh about 3 to 4 fish canes in one hour. SO, the manufacturing efficiency ensures that robots must help this fish manufacturing factory to raise fish canes number more than human workers. So, in robotic behavioral economy view, manufacturing robots must help this fish canes manufacturing factory to raise fish canes manufacturing number and deliver increasing number to supermarkets to prepare to sell every day. Robots can help this fish canes manufacturing factory bring manufacturing time saving, rising manufacturing efficiency, improving performance and reducing wages expenditure long time advantages in micro economy view. However, manufacturing robots can also bring disadvanages to society, e.g. increasing unemployment ratio, increasing crime rate,

this factory workers will lose jobs and income, they need earn social welfare from government and increasing government finance pressure in short time, even long time in macro economic view.

Stanford University graduate program in economics, Scott lecturer explained that "in demand and supply economic theory for robots supply and demand case, robots supply number increasing may influence human workers demand number decrease. It sometimes calls " the efficient frontier".

No specific human beings were mentioned in any of economics classes. As robots supply and demand in market case, They (robots) may be purely theoretical " agents" who reached to the most reasonable sale prices in order to persuade any one businessman buyer to make manufacturing robot buying decision whether robots can help him / her to bring how much saving time , saving money, saving cost, improving performance, efficiency economic benefit before he/she plans to reduce workers number when he/ she decides to apply robots to replace human workers in his/her factory or office or any service department, e.g. cinema ticket sale service, shopping center customer service, shopping center cleaning , supermarket customer service etc. service or sale tasks. When robots can replace human to do any one of these tasks in any organizations. So, robots may be human worker agents who reached to prices the way robots would react to a software

command. There was nothing that explained why some people thrived and others did n't or why truly brilliant, hardworking people could fail when much lazier folks succeeded." Having been admitted to the Stanford

University graduate program in economics, Scott lecturer hoped to get his answers there.

How robots influence our future social changing? Using the right technology can be a boon to your business in this economy. For internet example, it is easier than ever to find well-matched customers all around the world, to stay in contact with them, and to more quickly design the products they want. If you focus solely on being cutting -edge, though you risk letting the technology

take over what should be very robust relationships with your customers , employees, and colleagues. IN nowaddays society, technoligical advances and cutomation, personal

relationships in business are more crucial than ever. I mean that robots can not replace human to serve clients to let them to feel more comfortable and passion more easily. For shoe shop case example, if the shoe shop apply one robot to serve its clients to replace human shoe salesperson to serve its shoe customers. Robots ensure that they can not persuade every shoe potential buyer to make shoe buying decision more easily when robots need to contact every shoe potential buyer. The reason is simple, because robots can not touch any one shoe buyer individual emotion very easier.

If the shoe buyer needs the robots to help him/her to choose any right shoe styles when he/she can not feel himself / herself can make the most right shoe style choice decision. The robots can not replace human shoe salesperson to make shoe style choice judgement more easily. They must need longer time to analyze whether which shoe style may be the most suitable to the shoe buyer. Otherwise, human shoe salesperson may attempt to make the most right shoe style choice decision to help any one shoe buyer to chooce the most right style shoe because he/she owns shoe style sale experience, shoe style knowledge, the most important reason is that they can feel every shoe customer individual emotion to touch whether he/she will feel comfortable or happy when they attempt to help every shoe customer to seek the most right shoe style in every shoe customer whole shoe searching processing. Othwerwise, serving robots are only one machine, they can not touch or feel every shoe customer individual emotion whether he/she feel comfortable or unhappy or happy when they need to contact them in whole shoe searching processing. Hence, I believe that some tasks robots can

not repalce human staff to do very easily. Otherwise, robots may bring disadvanatges to let any one businessman to loss his/her customers, due to

robots can not touch every customer
emotion to compare human staff in service tasks more easily. Robots serving customer behaviors may cause money lose and customers number lose to the shop in micro economic view.

On conclusion, in demand and supply economic theory for robots supply and demand case, robots supply number increasing may influence human workers demand number decrease. So, it seems that robots number supply will be depended on global robots supply number more than robots demand number because when human began to accept robots to replace human to do general simple jobs in global labor market. Then, it means that global robots labor number must need to be increased in order to satisfy global businessmen workers number need. If any kinds of robot workers manufacture number is not enough to be supplied to let global future businessmen to buy, then robot supply will be shortage and they can not provide to satisfy global businessmen robots labour purchase need. So, future robot number will be depended on supply more than demand.

CHAPTER THREE

Human intellectual demand and supply behavior relationship

Intellectual human economic behaviors

What does intellectual human economic behaviors mean ? Human foolish behavior is depended on social enjoyment need more or material social supply more? I believe that when we choose or decide to do intellectual behaviors, then our societies will be influenced to bring economic growth in consequence.I shall attempt to indicate pollution case to explain how and why eithet our intellectual or foolish behaviors may bring economic growth or recession in consequence as below:

On one hand, for air pollution social case aspect example, if we only consider to buy cars to drive for working aim or holiday leisure aim. Then, our societies air will be polluted. Our health will be influenced to bad. Our car driving behaviors may cause global environment air pollution serously. In long tiem, global air pollution will bring our bodies health to be bad. Although, ourselves car driving behaviors may bring our driving travelling leisure enjoyment and comfortable feeling in short time, also we so not need to pay public transport fare often, but we need to compensate ourselves health economic intangible loss due to air pollution , when cars number increases, dirty air will cause ouselves health to become bad.

In the result, we will need to pay more medical expenditure when we are old age, due to ourselves bodies will become bad, due to we breathe global dirty air every day, due to ourselves cars pollute air in long time, e.g. 10 to 20 years, even 30 more without limited air pollution environment. So, driving cars behavior may be one kind of human foolish behavior and our foolish behavior may bring ourselves future long time medical expenditure absolutely.

One the other hand, water pollution social aspect, if we often keep much rubblish to pollute sea, oil exploration porcessing pollute ocean , ships gas pollute ocaen, then fishes will eat polluted food and drive dirty water, due to global ocean is polluted.

In fact, because human only to conside how to buy boats to carry on leisure enjoyment activities, or catch cruises to travel on the sea. Also, oil manufacturers only consider researching anywhere to find new oil exploration places to manufacture oil product, when their oil exploration processes pollute ocarn . Consequently, global fishes drink polluted warer or eat polluted food. They will have poison. SO, human will have high chance to eat poison polluted fishes, due to fishes are poison or are polluted. So, human is doing foolish activities, we only hope to find oil exploration places to pollute ocean or we only spend money to buy ticket to catch ships to travel anywhere in global ocean. All of these human foolish behaviors will bring pollution to global ocean. On consequently, we will need to compensate to eat polluted or dirty or poision fishes, ourselves bodies health will be bad. In long time, we need have high chance to pay medical expenditure when we are old. So, pollution case may be one good example to explain how and why human foolish behavior may influence ourselves future need to compensate serious medical loss.

All of these human foolish behavior will bring pollution to global ocean. On consequently, we will need to compensate to eat polluted or dirty or poison fished , ourselves bodies health will be bad. In long time, we will have high chance to pay medical expenditure, when we are old. So, pollution case may be one good example to explain how and why human ourselves intellectual or foolish behaviors may influence future long time economic loss or economic growth or recession in micro and micro economic view.

On another water pollution aspect hand, if we often keep rubbish to sea, oil exploration processing pollutes ocean and ships' gas pollute ocean, then fishes will eat polluted food and drink dirty water, due to fishes will eat polluted food and drink dirty sea water because the global ocean is polluted seriously.

In fact, because human only consider how to buy boats to carry on any leisure water activities, or catches cruises to travel on the sea. Also, oil manufacturers only consider any where to find oil exploratin places to manufacture oil products from ocean, when their pol exploration processes can plooute ocean. Consequently, global fishes drink polluted water or eat direty food. They will have poison. So, human will have high chance to eat poison fishes.

Otherwise, such as pollutin case, it can infuence inflation or deflation. Consequently, the reason indicates supply and demand theory. If air pollution is serious, then we will consider health issue, global cars demand number may be influenced to reduce, when global cars number demand will reduce, global car prices and supply number will need to change to fall down in order to attract or persuade global car consumers choose to make car purchase decision.

Hence, global car manufacture number and car price will be influenced to reduce, due to global air pollution issue. Consequently, deflation will occur because when the country citizen usually does not spend much extra saving money to buy car expensive goods. Money value will be low. Otherwise, if global cair pollution is not serious, human considers to buy cars to enjoy driving leisure lives. So, global car demand is influenced to increase , also global car price will also influenced to increase.

Consequently, gobal human will choose to buy cars to drive. Due to we accept to spend extra saving to buy expensive car goods. Car sale price and supply may be influenced to rise up. Money value is influenced to reduce. Inflation may be influenced, due to global car consumers number increases, we would not have extra money to spend easily. Car expensive goods expenditure influences our spending habit to avoid to make car purchase decision more easily. So, human intellectual or foolish activities may bring inflation or deflation consequency in possible indirectly in macro economic view.

On conclusion, above pollution case explain that how and why human intellectual or foolish economic behaviors may bring inflation or deflation consequency as wll as economic growth or recession consequency as well as any goods demand and supply increasing or decreasing consequency. It implies that human behavior may have indirect relationship to influence any goods demand and supply number to either increase or decrease result as well as any goods price will be influenced to increase or decrease in micro and macro economic view. Hence, Human foolish behavior is depended on social enjoyment need more or material social supply more because human needs to raise enjoyment feel , so we will choose to do foolish behavior, e.g. air pollution, when many people choose to buy cars to drive to replace catch public transport. So, such as car market, it depends on car demand number more than car supply number absolutely in demand and supply view.

The relationship between social change and human behavior

Why does economic changes may influence human individual behavioral change? I shall attempt to indicate shopping behavior and staying at home behavior to explain their case and effect relationsip as below:

Human behavior can be influenced by economic change or economic change can be influenced by human behavior? Why does recession may influence consumers reduce shopping desire? In social recession suitation, it is possible that many people lose jobs suddenly, due to businessmen lose many customers. They need to make decision to reduce employees number in order to continue to keep businesses. Consequently, many firms (organizations) their employees may lose jobs. When they have much time, due to lose jobs, they will feel to avoid to spend too much time and money to go to shopping often. Many losing jobs people, they will often stay at homes. So, they will reduce time to go to shopping, then non essential products won't their preferable choice purchase products. Hence, recession will change many losing jobs people their shopping or consumption desires to avoid to buy non essential products often . Usually when economic boom, many people have jobs to do because consumers number must increase when many people have jobs to do. Then, many people can accept to spend money to buy non essential products oftcn. Many pcople feel spend time to go to shopping can satisfy their purchase of any kinds of new products useful psychology or desire. So, recession is one good example to explain it can influence many people do not like often to leave homes to go to shopping easily. Many people like to stay at homes, becaue they feel worry about spending too much shopping time when they leave homes. Their staying home time is one good negative shopping behavior example. So, economic change may influence human individual behavior changes , they have direct cause and efect relationship in behavioral economic view.

May human behavior influence economic change? Is it possible that human behavior may bring the country social economic change in macro economic or micro behavioral economic view ? I shall indicate publishing industry example. Do you feel that if there are many students feel learning is very important when they read many books or many of students feel interesting to read or they have reading new books in habit, then it is possible that the country will have many students like to spend time to go to any book shops to choose the books, they feel that they can help they learn new knowledge. Then the country will increase students number, they often spend time to visit any one book shop every week. Their visiting book shops behavior which may become their habits. So, the country will increase students number, they often spend time to visit book shops. Also, it implies that visiting book shops behaviors may be their behavioral habits.

So, when the country has many students often spend time to visit book shops , their visiting book shops behaviors may help any one book shop to raise books sale chance. So, the country's student individual often visiting book shop behaviors, their habitual visiting book shops behaviors must may assist help any one book shop to increase books sale number absolutely.

Consequently, any one book shop , its books sale bumber must be influenced to increase to increase because the country will have many students like or feel need visit book shops habit in order to choose any suitable books to buy to read at home in order to raise themselves learning effort. When the country has many bok shops often have many students visit their book shops, then their books sale number may be influenced to increase. It explain why student individual visiting book shop behavior may help any one book shop sale number increases also. So, visiting shops products sale number is depended on online products supply number, if online products supply number increases, then it may cause many customers choose to buy the kind of products from online webstore. So, any shop products sale number will depend on onlint products supply number in supply and demand view.

CHAPTER FOUR

Technology or human behavior whether may influence economic growth or recession

Human Behavioral network job brings social economic benefits

What does human network job mean ? Why may human network job be popular? Why human network job behavior may influence economy ?

Nowadays internet is popular to use. We can apply internet to find data , search any new things, even earn money. Why does internet

may become huma network job source. For example, e-publish may be one kind of new human network job. Any authors may apply internet

channel to help them to sell electronic or paper books from e-publisher web store. They may apply facebook, you tub etc. any online

channel to promote themselves new books to let new readers to know whether when they may buy themselves favourable new topic books to read from electronic publisher web store.

Thus, future electronic publisher industry may help any authors to build internet network platform to help them to sell and promote

ot advertise their any one new electronic or paper book topic to let global any one reader to choose to buy their any new topic books from electronic publisher web store easily and conveniently. However, it implies that electronic network platform author may be one kind of future new human network job in our societies.

How electronic network platform author job may bring economy benefit in macro economy view? A person can have few friends, contacts and still be very influential if these few

friends and contacts are themselves highly influential, e.g. one author must not need to know any one reader in global society. When they like to choose any electronic books from electronic internet network platform. They may become the author's any one topic book buyer, when they feel the author's any one topic book is fun and attract they make decision to buth the strange author whose the topic book from electronic book publisher's platform web store conventiently in short time. Although, they are strangers, they do not know themselves , but the reader can understand what it way that made Google from writing platofrm to create new creative mind and typing network job method to replace traditional hand writing book method for global authors. It will be one kind of new human network writing job.

Hence, global any one reader can apply an innovative search engine , such as google.com to find whether whom author personal new topic books are value to read from internet.

Then, the electroniuc publisher's web store may be new book store platform sale network to help the author to sell many electronic or paper books from electronic network platform

in short time. So, internet may be future new network plaform to help global any one author to create network writing job absolutely. Furthermore, internet may be popular social media

to help any one author to build goold relationship between his/her readers. It is one kind of new network, human network job. New authors do not need to buy many paper books to prepare to put in any one book shop warehouse. Their every book can print on demand to reduce out of book stock in any one book shop. They may choose to sell either electronic books or paper books both from any one book publisher web store. So, electronic network platform may be one kind of good writing channel to help human authors to create income and it can also help authors to bring new creative mind and new topic fun content books to let readers to know and buy to read from electronic publisher network platform.

Why does human behavior may be one kind of new human network job to bring global economic advantages. ALthough, it may be free income or without inocme, but the person does the network behavior, his/her behavior may be bring advantages to influence many other people's health. For this case, when a worker in a coffee shop in an airport gets a vaccination aganinst the flu, it does not only helps him or her stay healthy, but also helps the many travellers who might otherwise have been inflected if that workers caught the flu. So, the externality , the result implies the vaccination of even a part of a community conveys benefits to the whole community. For example, governments pay special attention to the vaccinations of school children, teachers, health mothers, and the elderly, categories of people particularly susceptible not only to catching, but also to transmitting a disease.

It is not accidental that governments are heavily involved with vaccination . When there are externalities, free market, fail to persuade individual incentives with society's

their the worker's decision of whether to get a vaccine ends up attracting whether other people get sick. The workers might not fully take all these other people's potential suffering into account when making her or his vaccination decision.

As Stanford University does many suggestions, understand this and tries to help them make the right decisions and so providers free flu vaccines for its staff and students.

Small pockets of unvaccinated individuals can allow a disease to gain a spread more widely well-being. For example, parent weighing the costs and benefits of a vaccine for their child is not always thinking of the consequences of that vaccination to other people. THese are markets in which subsidizing or regulating behavior can make everyone better off. Because the reason for requiring that a child be vaccinated before enrolling in school is not just to protect that child, because each child's vaccination affects others via potential contagions.

Robots take our jobs behavioral and economy influences

Robot job behavior brings economy influences

If one day robots can replace human to do simple, even complex jobs. They will bring what influences to our global societial economy.The popular economic refrain declares that the

global middle class is dying and robots will soon take our jobs, e.g. shopping center customer service jobs, library service jobs, cinema ticket sale jobs, restaurant kitchen cooker jobs,

even, bus drivers, taxi drivers etc. public transport driving jobs, accountant, doctors etc. professional jobs. Whether it is beautiful or petty matter if our future societies have many human jobs can be replaced to do from robots.

Businessman must may reduce to employ employees and reduce to pay salary or wage, when robots can be replaced to do their employees tasks. But, societies must bring unemployement rate rises , due to societies will have many people loss jobs when their employers choose to buy robots to serve their clients or do any office tasks or customer service or cleaning etc. tasks.

In micro economy view, employers may save money in long term, but in macro economy view, it will cause unemployment ratio rises , even crime rate rises when there are many people lose
jobs in societies. These models of doom, though, fail to account for the hundreds of businesses riding the waves of change in their industries when robots may be invented to replace human to do many simple , even complex tasks in our future societies.

WE may image that one small factory needs to manufacture fishes canes to sell to supermarket, the small , cheaper stuff and higher margin parts of the fishes manufacture industry. Before, this factory needs to employe many human factory workers need to help every fresh customer makeing the perfect fishing gear, designed for performance, durability, and cost in order to achieve to manufacture every fish cane in whole fished processing manufacturing stages. Every worker needs to spend about 15 to twenty minutes to finish every fish cane , till to delivery to any supermarket to sell. If this fish canes manufacturing factory can apply manufacturing robots to help them to finish any one working tasks , every robot can only spend five minutes to finish whole fresh fish cane manufacturing process. Thus, every robot can
help this factory save 10 to 15 minutes time to finsh every fish cane manufacturing process. IN fact, time is money, because when every robot can help this factory to reduce 10 to 15 minutes time to compare human worker. Then, this factory can finish about 20 fish canes in one hour if it can use robot to help it to manufacture fish canes. Otherwise, if this factory still use human workers to help it to manufacture fish canes, then it can finsh about 3 to 4 fish canes in one hour. SO, the manufacturing efficiency ensures that robots must help this fish manufacturing factory to raise fish canes number more than human workers. So, in robotic behavioral economy view, manufacturing robots must help this fish canes manufacturing factory to raise fish canes manufacturing number and deliver increasing number to supermarkets to prepare to sell every day. Robots can help this fish canes manufacturing factory bring manufacturing time saving,

rising manufacturing efficiency, improving performance and reducing wages expenditure long time advantages in micro economy view. However, manufacturing robots can also bring disadvanages to society, e.g. increasing unemployment ratio, increasing crime rate,
this factory workers will lose jobs and income, they need earn social welfare from government and increasing government finance pressure in short time, even long time in macro economic view.

Stanford University graduate program in economics, Scott lecturer explained that "in demand and supply economic theory for robots supply and demand case, robots supply number increasing may influence human workers demand number decrease. It sometimes calls " the efficient frontier".
No specific human beings were mentioned in any of economics classes. As robots supply and demand in market case, They (robots) may be purely theoretical " agents" who reached to the most reasonable sale prices in order to persuade any one businessman buyer to make manufacturing robot buying decision whether robots can help him / her to bring how much saving time , saving money, saving cost, improving performance, efficiency economic benefit before he/she plans to reduce workers number when he/she decides to apply robots to replace human workers in his/her factory or office or any service department, e.g. cinema ticket sale service, shopping center customer service, shopping center cleaning , supermarket customer service etc. service or sale tasks. When robots can replace human to do any one of these tasks in any organizations. So, robots may be human worker agents who reached to prices the way robots would react to a software
command. There was nothing that explained why some people thrived and others did n't or why truly brilliant, hardworking people could fail when much lazier folks succeeded." Having been admitted to the Stanford University graduate program in economics, Scott lecturer hoped to get his answers there.

How robots influence our future social changing? Using the right technology can be a boon to your business in this economy. For internet example, it is easier than ever to find well-matched customers all around the world, to stay in contact with them, and to more quickly design the products they want. If you focus solely on being cutting -edge, though you risk letting the technology
take over what should be very robust relationships with your customers , employees, and colleagues. IN nowaddays society, technoligical advances

and cutomation, personal

relationships in business are more crucial than ever. I mean that robots can not replace human to serve clients to let them to feel more comfortable and passion more easily. For shoe shop case example, if the shoe shop apply one robot to serve its clients to replace human shoe salesperson to serve its shoe customers. Robots ensure that they can not persuade every shoe potential buyer to make shoe buying decision more easily when robots need to contact every shoe potential buyer. The reason is simple, because robots can not touch any one shoe buyer individual emotion very easier.

If the shoe buyer needs the robots to help him/her to choose any right shoe styles when he/she can not feel himself / herself can make the most right shoe style choice decision. The robots can not replace human shoe salesperson to make shoe style choice judgement more easily. They must need longer time to analyze whether which shoe style may be the most suitable to the shoe buyer. Otherwise, human shoe salesperson may attempt to make the most right shoe style choice decision to help any one shoe buyer to chooce the most right style shoe because he/she owns shoe style sale experience, shoe style knowledge, the most important reason is that they can feel every shoe customer individual emotion to touch whether he/she will feel comfortable or happy when they attempt to help every shoe customer to seek the most right shoe style in every shoe customer whole shoe searching processing. Othwerwise, serving robots are only one machine, they can not touch or feel every shoe customer individual emotion whether he/she feel comfortable or unhappy or happy when they need to contact them in whole shoe searching processing. Hence, I believe that some tasks robots can

not repalce human staff to do very easily. Otherwise, robots may bring disadvanatges to let any one businessman to loss his/her customers, due to robots can not touch every customer

emotion to compare human staff in service tasks more easily. Robots serving customer behaviors may cause money lose and customers number lose to the shop in micro economic view.

Intellectual human economic behaviors

What does intellectual human economic behaviors mean ? I believe that when we choose or decide to do intellectual behaviors, then our societies will be influenced to bring economic growth in consequence.I shall attempt to indicate pollution case to explain how and why eithet our intellectual or foolish behaviors may bring economic growth or recession in consequence as below:

On one hand, for air pollution social case aspect example, if we only consider to buy cars to drive for working aimr or holiday leisure aim. Then, our societies air will be polluted. Our health will be influenced to bad. Our car driving behaviors may cause global environment air pollution serously. In long tiem, global air pollution will bring our bodies health to be bad. Although, ourselves car driving behaviors may bring our driving travelling leisure enjoyment and comfortable feeling in short time, also we so not need to pay public transport fare often, but we need to compensate ourselves health economic intangible loss due to air pollution , when cars number increases, dirty air will cause ouselves health to become bad.

In the result, we will need to pay more medical expenditure when we are old age, due to ourselves bodies will become bad, due to we breathe global dirty air every day, due to ourselves cars pollute air in long time, e.g. 10 to 20 years, even 30 more without limited air pollution environment. So, driving cars behavior may be one kind of human foolish behavior and our foolish behavior may bring ourselves future long time medical expenditure absolutely.

One the other hand, water pollution social aspect, if we often keep much rubblish to pollute sea, oil exploration porcessing pollute ocean , ships gas pollute ocaen, then fishes will eat polluted food and drive dirty water, due to global ocean is polluted.

In fact, because human only to conside how to buy boats to carry on leisure enjoyment activities, or catch cruises to travel on the sea. Also, oil manufacturers only consider researching anywhere to find new oil exploration places to manufacture oil product, when their oil exploration processes pollute ocarn . Consequently, global fishes drink polluted warer or eat polluted food. They will have poison. SO, human will have high chance to eat poison polluted fishes, due to fishes are poison or are polluted. So, human is doing foolish activities, we only hope to find oil exploration places to pollute ocean or we only spend money to buy ticket to catch ships to travel anywhere in global ocean. All of these human foolish behaviors will bring pollution to global ocean. On consequently, we will need to compensate to eat polluted or dirty or poision fishes, ourselves bodies health will be bad. In long time, we need have high chance to pay medical expenditure when we are old. So, pollution case may be one good example to explain how and why human foolish behavior may influence ourselves future need to compensate serious medical loss.

All of these human foolish behavior will bring pollution to global ocean. On consequently, we will need to compensate to eat polluted or dirty or poison fished , ourselves bodies health will be bad. In long time, we will have high chance to pay medical expenditure, when we are old. So, pollution case may be one good example to explain how and why human ourselves intellectual or foolish behaviors may influence future long time economic loss or economic growth or recession in micro and micro economic view.

On another water pollution aspect hand, if we often keep rubbish to sea, oil exploration processing pollutes ocean and ships' gas pollute ocean, then fishes will eat polluted food and drink dirty water, due to fishes will eat polluted food and drink dirty sea water because the global ocean is polluted seriously.

In fact, because human only consider how to buy boats to carry on any leisure water activities, or catches cruises to travel on the sea. Also, oil manufacturers only consider any where to find oil exploratin places to manufacture oil products from ocean, when their pol exploration processes can plooute ocean. Consequently, global fishes drink polluted water or eat direty food. They will have poison. So, human will have high chance to eat poison fishes.

Otherwise, such as pollutin case, it can infuence inflation or deflation. Consequently, the reason indicates supply and demand theory. If air pollution is serious, then we will consider health issue, global cars demand number may be influenced to reduce, when global cars number demand will reduce, global car prices and supply number will need to change to fall down in order to attract or persuade global car consumers choose to make car purchase decision.

Hence, global car manufacture number and car price will be influenced to reduce, due to global air pollution issue. Consequently, deflation will occur because when the country citizen usually does not spend much extra saving money to buy car expensive goods. Money value will be low. Otherwise, if global cair pollution is not serious, human considers to buy cars to enjoy driving leisure lives. So, global car demand is influenced to increase , also global car price will also influenced to increase.

Consequently, gobal human will choose to buy cars to drive. Due to we accept to spend extra saving to buy expensive car goods. Car sale price and supply may be influenced to rise up. Money value is influenced to reduce. Inflation may be influenced, due to global car consumers number increases, we would not have extra money to spend easily. Car expensive goods expenditure influences our spending habit to avoid to make car purchase decision more easily. So, human intellectual or foolish activities may bring inflation or deflation consequency in possible indirectly in macro economic view.

On conclusion, above pollution case explain that how and why human intellectual or foolish economic behaviors may bring inflation or deflation consequency as wll as economic growth or recession consequency as well as any goods demand and supply increasing or decreasing consequency. It implies that human behavior may have indirect relationship to influence any goods demand and supply number to either increase or decrease result as well as any goods price will be influenced to increase or decrease in micro and macro economic view.

The relationship between social change and human behavior

Why does economic changes may influence human individual behavioral change? I shall attempt to indicate shopping behavior and staying at home behavior to explain their case and effect relationsip as below:

Human behavior can be influenced by economic change or economic change can be influenced by human behavior? Why does recession may influence consumers reduce shopping desire? In social recession suitation, it is possible that many people lose jobs suddenly, due to businessmen lose many customers. They need to make decision to reduce employees number in order to continue to keep businesses. Consequently, many firms (organizations) their employees may lose jobs. When they have much time, due to lose jobs, they will feel to avoid to spend too much time and money to go to shopping often. Many losing jobs people, they will often stay at homes. So, they will reduce time to go to shopping, then non essential products won't their preferable choice purchase products. Hence, recession will change many losing jobs people their shopping or consumption desires to avoid to buy non essential products often . Usually when economic boom, many people have jobs to do because consumers number must increase when many people have jobs to do. Then, many people can accept to spend money to buy non essential products often. Many people feel spend time to go to shopping can satisfy their purchase of any kinds of new products useful psychology or desire. So, recession is one good example to explain it can influence many people do not like often to leave homes to go to shopping easily. Many people like to stay at homes, becaue they feel worry about spending too much shopping time when they leave homes. Their staying home time is one good negative shopping behavior example. So, economic change may influence human individual behavior changes , they have direct cause and efect relationship in behavioral economic view.

May human behavior influence economic change? Is it possible that human behavior may bring the country social economic change in macro economic or micro behavioral economic view ? I shall indicate publishing industry example. Do you feel that if there are many students feel learning is very important when they read many books or many of students feel interesting to read or they have reading new books in habit, then it is possible that the country will have many students like to spend time to go to any book shops to choose the books, they feel that they can help they learn new knowledge. Then the country will increase students number, they often spend time to visit any one book shop every week. Their visiting book shops behavior which may become their habits. So, the country will increase students number, they often spend time to visit book shops. Also, it implies that visiting book shops behaviors may be their behavioral habits.

So, when the country has many students often spend time to visit book shops , their visiting book shops behaviors may help any one book shop to raise books sale chance. So, the country's student individual often visiting book shop behaviors, their habitual visiting book shops behaviors must may assist help any one book shop to increase books sale number absolutely.

Consequently, any one book shop , its books sale bumber must be influenced to increase to increase because the country will have many students like or feel need visit book shops habit in order to choose any suitable books to buy to read at home in order to raise themselves learning effort. When the country has many bok shops often have many students visit their book shops, then their books sale number may be influenced to increase. It explain why student individual visiting book shop behavior may help any one book shop sale number increases also.

How human productive behavior may influence economic development

May any country which citizen behavior assist themselves country development? It is one cause and effect economic question. I mean that if the country itself citicen can not concentrate mind or energy to choose to do one kind of industry in order to let themselves country can bring the most benefit, then whether the counry itself economy can bring the most serious economic benefit. I shall attempt to indicate these countries themselves indistry choice to explain whether these countries themselves citizen productive behavior may help themselves countries to achieve the largest economic benefits. I shall indicate as below:

New Zealand farmer individual wine productive behavior

For New Zealand country example, this country concerns itself effort is foucs on farming agricultural aspect. So, this country has many farmers concentrate on farming agricultural aspect. May New Zealanders choose to spend time to produce different kinds of wines, e.g. wine or red grape wine is for the people are eating meat, or they are eating dinner.

When these New Zealanders their behaviors choose to do farming or agriculture to grow and produce different kinds of taste of white or red grape wine drinking products job. Themselves grape agriculture behavior will influence these New Zealanders themselves, they can learn how to improve different kinds of grape wine drinking products in order to achieve every kinds of white or read grape wines taste improving aim during their white or red grape producing process.

Why can New Zealander every individual white or read grape wine producers improve their white or read grape wine taste more easily? In behavioral economic view, it can explain that why any one New Zealander white or read grape wine producer can be encouraged or excited or persuaded to concentrate nervous and energy and effort to learn how to improve their white or red grape wine products easily.

In fact, New Zealand is one agricultural food export country. It has good natural environment resource , e.g. land, seed to provide any one farmer to produce themselves any kinds of agricultrual food products, e.g. fruit, or wine food products. Because New Zealanders know themselves country has enough natural resource . So, in common, many New Zealanders choose to attempt to do farming agricultural jobs in order to export themselves any kinds of fruit or meat or wine products to overseas or sell to domestic in order to earn profit.

So, when these New Zealand farmers number has been increasing every year. This country farmers will feel themsleves competition between this New Zealand farmers themselves are serious due to they may feel New Zealanders choose to do agriculture businesses in order to export themselves different kinds of farming food to overseas or sell to local to earn profit.

Hence, when many New Zealand farmers feel that farmers number has been increasing every year. They will feel themselves competition is serious. They must need to spend much time and nervous and effort to research what method is the best how to produce the best taste of white or red grape wine products in order to let local or overseas wine buyers to choose to buy his/her producing white or read grpae products to drink.

Hence, in competition psychological view, may influence many New Zealand white or reaad wine producers had been beginning to change their learning behavior on researching what method is the best in order to produce the best quality of taste red or white wine products to sell in order to attract overseas or local white or read grape wine drinkers to choose to buy his/her wine products. Their behavior will focus on learning how to raising or improving white or read grape wine taste method more than only focus on producing a large number white or red grape wine products. They believe wine quality is more important to compare wine producing number. So, New Zealand wine producers themselves wine producers behaviors have been changing on concentrating on researching wine quality method aspect more then wine producing number aspect in behavioral economic view.

America high technological productive behavior

For America example, US is one high technological country, it owns many high technological knowledge talent inventors, e.g. computer science inventors. Hence, US must attract many diferent countries owning high technological computer inventors choose to go to US to develop their computer science profession career. Also, it seems that when many computer science inventors or professions choose to go to US to develop themselves computer science new career. In behavioral economic view, due to their leaving themselves countries choice, which may bring influence themselve country job behaviors need to be changed. They must need to adapt US new live. Because they will forgive their past computer science job. These computer science professionals need to spend time to adapt US new lives. They " past computer science job behaviors" will need to be changed to their new US any computer employer's new computer science job model.

Because their traditional computer science jobs needed to be forgot in their themselves countries. They will feel their old computer science job knowledge and behavior needed to change in order to let their US any one new of computer company employer feels satisfactory to accept their new working behavior in any one US computer organization.

So, on the other hand, many US computer company employer will feel that they must need time to accept any one new overseas computer science professions their working behaviors, their working attitude daily, because these foreign comouter science professional, their past computer working behaviors and working attitude must be different to US domestic computer science professions.

In behavioral economic view, these overseas computer science professions, their working behaviors and attitude must be needed to change in order to adapt any one US new computer company itself domestic or local computer science professional stafs themselves daily working behaviors and attitude because these overseas and local computer science professionals must need to team work together.

In behavioral economic view, it is only one way that foreign computer science professionals must need to change themselves past country traditiona daily working behaviors and attitude in order to cooperate with these US local computer science professionals in teams more easily.

Consequently, if these foreign compute science professionals can change their past working behaviors and attitude to let any one US local computer science professional feels to cooperate with them easily in short time. Then, the US computer company itself whole computer professional teams themselves efficiencies will be influenced to raised or improved by the changing past working attitude and working behaviors of these foreign computer science professionals. So, in behavioral economic view, only if US any one computer company hopes itself computer teams themselves efficiency can be raised or improved when it decides to employ foreign computer science professionals and US domestic computer science professionals. They need to work in teams together. They must need to let these foreign computer science professionals to know how to change their working behaviors and attitude to let their domestic computer science professionals feel easy to work together. Then, the US computer company itself whole team efficiency must be rasied or improved easily in short time.

● China share market investing behavior

For China share market example, economic development depends on financial market. Because if many Chinese have interest to invest to carry on shares buying and selling activities in orde to learn how to earn shares interest and share profit when the China shareholder can make decision to sell himself/herself shares in the the high price, then he/she can earn money when he/she can sell the China company's shares in the high sale share price position.

If China has many Chinese like to spend time to carry on investing shares activities. Themselves shares buying and selling behaviors will influence China has many companies can increase fund from many Chinese shareholders in order to have enough money to expand or develop themselves businesses in China in long term.

Consequently, when China can have many Chinese like to attempt to carry on buying and selling shares investing behaviors in China share market. Themselves buying and selling shares behaviors can help many Chinese companies have effort to increase enough money or capital in order to continue to do their businesses in long term absolutely. So, it explains why when many Chinese become shareholders , they can assist China will have many companies continue to develop their businesses if many Chinese like to carry on shares buying and selling investing behaviors in long time in China financial investment market nowadays in behavioral economic view.

Why has any individual country have many people invest share behavior which can influence the country's macro consumption desire?

I shall apply shares market buying and selling investment behavior to explaiin why shares investment behavior which may impact the country's overal consumption desire as below:

In behavioral economic view, I assume that when the coutry has many people have interest to attempt to carry on shares buying and selling investment behavior, then their frequent shares buying and selling behaviors which may bring negative consumption desire or shopping desire of these shares investors their consumer behavior.

The reason is simple, when the country has many share buyers number suddenly been increasing rapidly. Consequently, these large group share investors must need to spend much time to research any kinds of company shares variations, whether when their share prices will rise up of fall down in order to achieve buying the company's shares in the lowest price and selling the company's shares in the highest price level in order to earn profit.

Basic on this reason, they must need to spend much extra time to research share prices changing behavior every day, e.g. one working person will wait to leave his/her job, after he/she can spend time to gather data to research the day's share price changing behavior after dinner. So, the working person's right time may be his/her share price market research behavior. Before he/she may spend his/her night time to go to shopping after dinner, but nowadays, he/she will fogive to do his/her shopping behavior before dinner or after dinner at hight sometime. He/she will make decision to spend much night time to turn on computer to click on share market website to research his/her share purchase choice to investigate whether his/her share price whether it rises up or falls down at the moment in order to make his/her share buying or selling decision at ever night time.

I mean the when the country has many people are share investors, their shares investment behavioral spenging time which will influence many shops lose customers at might often because the country will have many people feel need to spend night time to turn on computer or watch television to investigate share price variation. So, the country will have many people / share investors choose to stay at home in order to carry on share price variation investigation behavior, they need to listen share market update news from radios or watch the share market update news from computer or TV at home every night. Consequenly, they must reduce times to leave themselves homes at night. So, their shopping behavior also will be reduced. Because these share investors feel need to spend time to investigate share price variation news at homes which can bring economic benefits (high opportunity benefits) when they choose to forgive to leave homes to go to shopping times (opportunity cost) every night.

On conclusion, it seems that when the country has many people are share investors, then their share price investigating behavior may bring negative shopping emotion at night. Consequently, the country's any one shop may lose many customers from this share investor consumer group in behavioral economic view. Hence, when the country's share investors number had been increasing rapidly, it will influence any shops lose many customers from this share investing customer group at night frequenly in short time, even long time in behavioral economic view, because their shopping desires or shopping emotion will be brought negative feeling when they make decisions to spend much time to listen radios or watch TV or computers share price update nes at night. Hence, share market will bring negative impact to influence consumer shopping desire or negative shopping emotion in behavioral economic view.

Can technology influence human shopping behavioral change?
Nowadays, technological development has reached mature stage, whether technological mature stage may bring positive or negative shopping emotion influence to global consumers. I shall aplly internet inventin or ecommerce shopping channel tool to explain whether internet technology can bring postive or negative influence to global consumer behavior in behavioral economic view.
Internet is a good technological tool, it brings e-commerce business chance.

In fact, commonly, global has have many businessmen choose to use internet channel to carry on their products transactions between global online-buyers and their electronic websites. So, global many shoppers had begun to feel online shopping is more convenient to compare visiting shops shopping. Their shopping behaviors have been changed from internet technological tool. Global has many shoppers choose to buy any products from any overseas or local businessmen their web stores. They only need to spend time to find any businessmen their webstores to choose the most suitable products to pay visa to buy from their webstores. at homes. So, in general, global had have may shoppers had changed their shopping behaviors from visiting shops to visiting webstores at homes often.

So, it seems that internet technological tool had influenced global many shops disappear, but internet webstores will be replaced their actual shops on streets. Some of businessmen either they choose webstores to replace shops or choose websotes and shops both or still keep shops only. Hence, internet tool influences global businessmen have three kinds of products sale channels to let globa local and overseas consumers to choose how to buy their products.

However, in fact, many of global shoppers, youngers and olders had begun to accept to buy any products from webstores. They feel to spend time to leave homes to visit shops , their shopping behaviors will be wasted time to not essential part to their daily lives. Hence, since internet technological invention, it had changed many consumers their traditional visiting shops shopping habit to change to buying products from webstores channel.

However, on the one hand, internet creates webstores ecommerce shopping channel to let global many consumers do not need to leave homes to go to shopping. It brings negative visiting shops shopping emotion to global general consumers nowadays. But on the other hand, it also brings positive visiting internet webstores shopping emotion to global general consumer nowadays. So, it seems that global many consumers feel that they often do not need to spend much time to go out shopping. Many global consumers feel convenient and enjoy to choose any products to buy from different internet webstores, when the online buyer chooses the most suitable product, he she only needs to pay visa card to buy the product from the online seller's webstore conveniently at home.

Hence, online shopping can bring economic benefit to online buyers, e.g. avoiding walking time or spending transport fare to visit the shop to go to shopping, shortening or reducing shopping time to do another important matter.

On conclusion, global many consumers began feel online shopping can bring more economic benefits on shortening shopping time, avoiding transport fare spending aspect. So, online shopping will be popular shopping behavior for future long time. It may encourage global many shoppers can make rapid shopping decision in short time in order to carry on any products buying transaction to global any one online shopper in short time easily in behavioral economic view. So, global many businessmen had begun to build themselves one attraction webstore in order to persuade different countries consumers to choose to click themselves webstores from internet channel to buy any kinds of products in short time easily.

So, internet technology had changed consumers traditional shopping behaviors to build positive online shopping emotion as well as raise online sellers' any products sale chance easily in behavioral economic view.

Why and how human behavior may influence the country's economic growth or recession?

When one country has many people choose to do the same matter for one period, whether their behavior may influence the country's pvera; economic growth or recession . I shall attempt to indicate cases toexplain their relationship as below:

For flowing rubblish behavioral case example, do you feel that when the country has many people often flow rubblish on the streets, instead of their flowing rubblish behavior may bring streets dirty? But, their flowing rubblish behavior may explain that this country has people may have enough money to buy food to ear, or enough cloths to wear, enough bottles of water to drink, even they may have enough money to buy new television, radio, refrigeraters , washing machines, desktops or laptops electronic home products from old to new to use in order to satisfy their living needs. So, when they flow old electronic home products, their flowing old home electronic products behaviors may seem that they have enough money to buy other new home electronic products to replace old home electronic products to use at homes.

However, it seems thaat this country ought have many people have jobs to do. So, many of them, they can easy to make purchase decison to flow any old home electronic products and buy any new home electronic products to use . Because this country has many people have jobs to do. So, they can often not use old home electonic products to become rubblishs to flow on streets after they had bought any kinds of new home electronic homes.

In fact, it also implies that this country's economy grows rapidly. So, many businesses can glow up rapdly. When they expanded their businesses, they must need to increase employees number in order to let they help themselves to raise productivity or serve their clients absolutely. So, when the country has many businesses can grow up, it seems that its economy must be better or it is improved to compare past. Due to many different kinds of home electronic products had been often bought to use by this country people in this period. So, this country's any streets can be observed that expensive electronic home products were flowed on streets anywhere. then, this country will have many electronic home products sellers can sell their home electronic products very easily. When this country has many people can find any kinds of jobs to do easily. So, due to unemploymen rate had been decreasing.

In behavioral economic view, as this many electronic home products rubblish country case, we can observe this country may have many people have jobs to do. So, consumption number has been increased long time. So, cheap food, or expensive home electronic products may be rubblish on any streets. This country's people , their flowing rubblish behaviors may be explained that many of people have enough jobs to do, so they have ability to buy any good taste food to eat or buy any kinds of expensive electronic home products to use. So, this country's economy may be improved for this long period. So, in behavioral economic view, when this country can have many electronic home products rubblishs are flowed on anywherer in streets frequently. It seems that this country will have many people have jobs to do, so it causes they often change old home electronic products or replaced them easily, when they have enough income to spend to buy any kinds of new home electronic products to use at homes easily. Moreover, their flowing old electronic home products behaviors also indicate that this country has many people their salaries may be increased in possible from their emplyers. When this country can have many different kinds of home electornic products are sold. It means that this country's electronic home products needs or demand had been increasing, due to many people have jobs to do and income increases to excite their living of needs also improve. Consequently, this country may seem have better economic improvement. We can observe from this country's electronic home products rubblish increasing income in theis period.

On conclusion, this country ought experience economic growth at this period. So, " flowing expensive electronic home rubblish increasing number

" may seem that this country's economic growth is rapidly in this period, due to many people have jobs to do as well as salaries increase in this period.

Technology how impacts human behavior changing?
Technology how influences human behavior to bring changing? For example, online share purchase and sale transaction from smart phone brings share investor can do share buying or selling transation in any where and any time conveniently, non manual driving auto vehicle, bring car owner feels comfortable and spends free time to do other matter, e.g. reading, listening mucis in himself or herself car freely. electrical energy vehicle can help car owner to reduce air polluton and it can brings the drivers do not feel drive long time in any journeys in order to avoid air pollution for environmental protection responsible car drivers in our societies. Thus, they will drive long time in any journeys when they can drive electronic energy cars to replace oil energy cars.

However, online technology can also bring consumers can choose to stay at homes to buy any things from seller individual online webstore conveniently. Such as online technology can bring shoppers do not need to spend much time to visit shops to buy any things. They can choose any kinds of products from any online sellers individual online webstores conveniently at homes. Online technology excite busy consumers can make purchase decision easily as well as it can help online sellers sell any kinds of products from internet easily.

In behavioral economic view, technology can change human behavior to be improved, it can let human feels comfortable, more free time ro use, rapid making any decisions, such as apply smart phones to make share purchase or sale transaction decision, online shopping decision, even travelling any where decision in short time, when the traveller finds the most cheap hotel accommodation room price and air ticket price frm any travel agent online tourism webstore, then the potential travel customer can follow the online hotel accommodation price and air ticket price data to make decision when to buy the air ticket from the airline travel agent or make decision when to prebook which hotel accommodation room to go to the country to travel from online travel agent tourism webstores. So, technology can encourage global any country travelers to make anywhere to trvel rapidly. If the traveler can find the country's general hotel rooms and airline tickets prices had been decreasing more sightly. The traveler may make travel decision to choose the country to travel in short time, then he/she can prebook the country;s any hotel room and airline ticket to pay by visa fraom the country's any hotel and airline travel agent webstores., before one week, even one month or more easily. Hence, online technology can also encourage traveler individual frequent travel times to be increased, due to global travelers can find any hotel rooms and airline tickets prices from internet conveniently at homes. They do not need to spend time to visit any airline travel agent to enquire travel choice country's hotel rooms prices and airline ticket prices. They can compare global travel of countries choices ' all hotels rooms and airline agents air tickets prices to make prebook airline seat and hotel room decision before one week, one month even six months early.

On conclusion, online technology can encourage global travelers can make travelling any where and when traveling time desicions easily. It can excite tourism industry develops in long time. Also, such as electricity cars invention can encourage environment protection car owners do car purchase decision easily, because they can choose to drive electronic energy cars to replace oil energy cars in order to avoid air pollution occurs easily. So, electronic cars can increase electronic car purchasrs number, due to many of environmental protection attitude of car owners can choose to drive electricity cars to bring air cleans, even non -manual driving cars can encourage lazy driving and free time driving car owners to choose to buy non-manual (artificial intelligent) cars to drive , because they can spend much free time to read, listen music or do any matters in themselves cars, they do not need to drive cars, robotic (AI) auto driving machine is such one non-manual driver to help them to drive themselves cars confidently. So, non-manual driving cars can attract lazy and enjoying free time driving car owners to choose to buy to replace traditional manual cars to drive easily. Moreover, online share transaction can help any share investors to make share buying and selling decision in short time easily. When they can apply smart phones technological tool to carry on share buying and selling activities easily. They can observe any share rising or falling price suitation from smart phones in any where any any time easily. So, smart phone technology can help global any shareholders to make share purchase and sale transaction easily. So, technology can encourage human makes decision in short time rapidly.

How and why employees behaviors may influence economy development?

In behavioral economy view,I believe the country's any organizational employees behavior may bring indirect relationship to influence the country's long term economic development. I shall indicate past manufacture industry social development period to explain their relationship. For many countries' past business activities had belonged to manufacturing industry, such as US, UK past before 1980 year, it focused on steel manufacturing and steel manufacturing related machine products. So, US, Uk developed countries manufacturing industries may be past main country's economic income sources. I assume US , UK past had one million number different kinds of industries. They ought had about seven houndred thousand number organizational businesses were belonged to manufactured industry. They may include:

Steel manufacturing and steel related machine manufacturing, e.g. vehicle manufacturing, home appliances, e.g. washing machine, television, radio, refrigerate cooler, heater, air condition etc. different kinds of different kinds of steel -related manufacturing machine, they were manufactured from US, UK steel machine manufacturers. So, US, Uk the other three hundred thousand number industry may be general service industry, e.g. hotel service, restaurent, cinema, public transport service, tourism lesiure , wine bar, supermarket etc. different kinds of non-manufacturing industries business organizations were operated in UK, US past before 1980 year.

So, in UK, US developed countries industry development history, they ought have high percentage of businesses belonged to steel related manufacturing machine and steel products. Also, in the past before 1980 year, US, Uk business employers , they employed many workers are manufacturing workers. They needed to spend long time to work in factories. They were skillful workers, and they are trained to manufacturing cars, washing machine, television, heater, etc. even steel itself different kinds of steel related products to prepare to deliver to their shops to sell to US, Uk local or overseas clients.

So, I believe that past UK, US ought employ many employees, they belonged to skillful manufacturing workers, manufacture increasing steel machine or steel related machine number of products rapidly daily. So, if UK, US had had many of these manufacturing factories owned high skillful workers, then their manufacturing steel-related machine or steel both kinds of products number must be influenced to raise rapidly. Consequently, their steel machine manufacturing products would been exported to overseas or would been sold to local both markets , they may be influenced to raise sale number. They (these manufacturing workers) needed to be trained to know how to manufactur these different kinds of machine products in the efficient teams and they ought to be trained to raise their efficiencies in order to shorten time to manufacturing many kinds of steel related manufacturing machine or steel itself products rapidly. So , if their efficiencies and manufacturing performance was improved, these US, UK any one manufacturing worker and their teams ought achieve raising productivities significantly.

Hence, when past UK, US manufacturing industry development period, if these two countries' any manufacturing factories could have many manufacturing workers could be trained to be skillful and proficient manufacturing workers. Then, in past every day to these factories workers, they ought help their steel or steel related manufacturing employers to raise any kinds of machine or steel products number in every team. So, when past in the manufacturing industry development, US, UK could have many factories' manufacturing workers themselves steel or steel related machine products manufacturing skill could be trained to to improve to any kinds of these machine or steel manufacuring products quality as well as their products number could be influenced to raise by themselves skillful improvement significantly every day.

Then, what would be influenced to occur to past UK, US manufacturing industry period? In behavioral economic view, when these two manufacturing industry developed countries, such as UK, US , if they had many factories workers can be trained to improve their skill in order to achieve any kinds of steel or steel-related machine products quality could be improved as well as products manufacturing number could be also increased absolutely.

In consequence, past UK and US both countries ought increase themselves any kinds of steel and steel related machine products number to be supplied to themselves local shops to let local clients to choose any one kind of machine manufacturing products to buy easily as well as they could also export to supply overseas any countries to buy their different kinds of steel or steel related machine products to let overseas steel or steel related manufacturing machine product buyers, they can have many of these different kinds of these steel or steel-related different kinds of manufacturing machine from UK and UK these both countries easily to compare other countries.

On conclusion, I believe that past US, and UK macro manufacturing industry income GDP would increase significantly. So, they would have good economic growth performance because when many of these manufacturing workers themselves manufacturing effort could be improved. So, it explained when employees manufacturing abilities can influence economic growth indirectly.

Robots invention whether they can help organizations to raise efficiencies or inefficiencies?

In behavioral economic view, in any organizations, when the organization hopes its worker teams can raise efficiencies , the organization may choose to increase more workers number and/or it can provide training to improve these workets themselves skills in order to raise their efficiencies. For one warehouse example, when the warehouse increases many goods , they are needed to delivered these goods from the shelves to the delivering destination locations. If this warehouse supervisors feel these workers themselves goods delivery speeds are slow, which is possible due to this warehouse's workers number is not enough. So, this warehouse supervisor ought increase workers number in order to increase their goods delivery speed in order to deliver goods from the shelves to every indicated goods delivery destination in order to let any one lorry driver can transport the right kinds of goods and ensure the accurate goods number to transport to any one client home rapidly.

However, if this warehouse supervisor planed to buy several warehouse goods delivery robots to assist these warehouse workers to find the right kinds of goods from shelves and then deliver to the right destination location in the warehouse. So, these warehouse orkers can concentrate on counting the accurate goods number and ensuring the right kinds of goods in order to prepare to let lorry drivers to transport these goods to these goods of buyers themselvers homes rapidly. Consequently, in the first step, robots can concentrate on finding th right goods from shelves and delivers them to the right goods transportation of location destination. Then, in the second step, these warehouse workers can concentrate on counting the accurate goods number and ensuring the right kinds of goods in order to prepare to put them to the lorry. Consequently, when warehouse robots and warehouse workers can cooperate to work together, the most important, robots, can deal on finding the right kinds of goods and deal on delivering the accurate number of goods of job duty as well as these warehouse workers can only concentrte on counting the right kinds of goods number in order to avoid it has none any mistake of wrong kinds of goods and inaccurate goods of delivery number to be transported to the lorry and to deliver to any one buyer's home.

So, it seems that warehouse robots ought help any one warehouse worker to raise himself efficiency and avoid goods delivery of mistake occurrence easily as well as their help to warehouse workers that can let any one goods buyer feels their goods can be delivered to their homes rapidly. Moreover, warehouse robots can also help these warehouse workers to raise efficiencies because warehouse robots can help them to shorten goods delivery time between any one shelf and any one goods delivery destination of location in the warehuse because robots may help them to find the right kinds of goods from the right shelf in the short time. So, any one worker does not need to spend long time to seek anywhere is the right shelf location for the kind of goods when the kind of goods are needed to deliver to the buyer's home from lorry. Warehouse robots can help them to do this aspect of " finding the goods from the right shelf in short time job duty". So, any one warehouse worker only needed tospend less time to do the counting of any right kind of goods number and ensuring the right kind of goods job duty. Consequently, this warehouse 's any one worker, his any one kind of goods delivery time may be reduced, because robots' assistance and they may have more confidence to avoid mistake to deliver the wrong number of goods and/or the wrong kind of goods to any one goods buyer's home.

On conclusion, it seems that warehouse robots ought may help any one warehouse worker to raise efficiency for any one team in the warehouse as well as the warehouse any one supervisor does not need to spend much time to observe any one worker individual performance for " goods delivery job duty aspect" because their goods delivery job duty that had been replaced to do by these several warehouse robots. Robots can achieve the more accurate of right kinds of goods and the right number of goods delviery job performance to compare any one of human warehouse worker themselves right kinds of goods of delivery and right number of goods of delivery job performance. So, when robots can participate to cooperate with this warehouse's any one worker to do their goods of delivery job duty in this warehouse every day. Then, robots can raies any one of supervisor individual confidence in order to let they do not need to spend time to observe any one of worker individual whose goods of delivery job performane. They can concentrate on supervising any one worker whose goods transport to lorry in the final step in order to avoid to deliver wrong goods number and / or wrong kind of goods to any one goods buyer's home every day. Consequently, this warehouse's overall teams of their delviery of goods performance many be improved by robotss' participatin to goods of delivery task as well as this warehouse's oveall teams themselves efficiencies may be influenced to raise by robots' goods of delivery task participation.

Why social behavior may influence organizational strategy needs to be changed ?

Why any organizations need to know whether nowadays social behaivor how has been changing in order to implement the kind of the most right strategy to achieve the profit aim pursue in possible. I shall indicate nowadays ecommerce or online, customer shopping behavior to explain above question concerns they ought have close relationship between social behavior and organizational strategic choice or organizational behavioral changing need.

On nowadays ecommerce business, or online shopping model, this kind of shopping model in global many young and old age consumers like to apply internet tool to choose any country sellers website stores in order to stay at home to buy any kinds of products from themselves webstores in global societies.

In fact, online shopping model had been popular for long time above to twenty years. Most of global sellers will make decision to design themselves webstores in order to attract global many online buyers to choose to buy their products from themselves webstores. So, it seems that social consumers purchase behaviors had been changed to online shopping from internet invention.

Hence, social consumers purchase behavioral changes may influence any organizations' strategies need to be changed from visiting shops purchase strategy model to online purchase strategy model, if the seller still concentrate on concentrate on considerate how to design itelf , but neglects to considerate how to design itself webstore, e.g. how to design attract product photos to put on itself webstore, how to arrange sale price information location to be putted on webstore and visa card payment location on itself webstore in order to let any one online buyer can feel very easier to buy itself any kinds of products from itself webstore. Then, its potential online buyers will be influenced to increase number when they can find this online seller itself any kinds of products photes and every kinds of product sale price information and visa card payment channel locations easily from itself webstore.

So, it implies that nowadays any one seller ought need to design one webstore to let any one online overseas and domestic consumers can have chance to click itself webstore to choose any one kind of product to buy conveniently when he/she does not hope to leave him/her home to go to shop, because nowadays social shopping behaviors had been influenced to change when internet invention, them it gives another online purchase method to replace visiting shops purchase method to global any one buyer in nowadays societies.

So, if nowadays any one seller still concentrate on how to design itself shop display in order to put any kinds of product on shelf in order to let any one visiting shop customer to find the kind of product to buy, but it neglects to change to choose to pursue another new technological shopping method, such as webstore purchase method in order to implement effective strategy to design the most right webstore as well as in order to attract global overseas and local consumers to find itself webstore easily from website and find its any one kind of product phots and sale price and visa card payment button in order to choose to buy itself any kinds of products in the short time. Consequently I believe that the seller will lose many customers from overseas and local when its other same or similar product sellers choose to design themselves webstores in order to let global any one product buyer can buy themselves any one kind of product when they can pay visa card to buy their products from them webstores conveniently when they stay at home habitly. Then, the seller will lose many global potential customers in long time.

On conclusion, in behavioral economic view, any consumer behavioral social changing, which will influence any in order to avoid customers number loses significantly . In future time, organizations need to make rapid decision in order to implement the most reasonable and the most useful strategy in order to avoid global potential customers number reduces or lose them in long time. So, social behavioral changing environment ought influence any global organizations need to decide how to change themselves strategies in order to avoid customers loses significantly in future time.

How and why human behavior may influence economic growth or recession?

May ourselves daily behaviors influence our global societial continue economic growth or recession? Do they have cause and effect close relationship between human behaviors and global economic growth or recession? I shall apply behavioral economic theory to analyze and explain whether ourselves daily behaviors and our global societial economic growth or recession which have close cause and effect relationship as below:

Every country itself economic development must depend on any business activities, otherwise, any kinds of business activities must need ourselves business activities or behaviors in order to achieve any business activities as well as achieve the country's overall economic development in macro view. However, any country's overall business activites or behaviors which must depend on any kinds of individual businessmen, themselves employees daily working behavior or activity or performance in order to help them to attract or increase many clients number to acieve " earning profit" aim. So, it seems that any individual business, itself overall every department individual working behavior is one main factor to influence the company's overall business performance.

For agricultural fruit and meat food farming industry example, such as New Zealand is a farming main target industry country. It had had many New Zealanders were daily themselves own farming businesses for many years. Their farming businesses include growing fruit, sheep, cow, pig pork, meat etc. food sale business. If the New Zealand farmer owned a large size farming land, then he will choose either growing fruit or feeding sheeps, pigs, cows to be meat to to transport to New Zealand supermarkets to help them to sell to their farmers meet to New Zealanders in order to earn profit. Thus, if the New Zealand farmer owned large size of farming lands, then he needs to employ many farming employees (farming workers) to help him to carry on farming business daily tasks, e.g. picking up friuts, feeding pigs, cows, sheeps to eat food daily. These daily farming jobs are very important to influence this New Zealand farmer's meats or fruits sale number whether they can be easy or diffcult to sell in New Zealand supermarkets , if these farming workers can own encough farming knowledge or skill to know how to pick up fruits method and make judgement to know whether it is right time to pick up the kind of fruits from the trees , as well as know how feed this pigs, sheeps, cows to eat food in order to let they are better health. Consequently, their farming behaviors which can let these animals can provide the best taste and enough meat from these animals to let New Zealander to buy to eat from New Zealand any one supermarket. Even these New Zealand farming workers can know whether the kinds of fruits, e.g. oranges, apples, gapes etc. fruits whether they ought be picked up from the trees at the right time. Consequently, they can make judgement to decide to pick up any kinds of the best taste fruits to let any one New Zealander to buy to eat from any one supermarket in New Zealand. Otherwise, if they do not make judegement to know whether the kind of fruit ought not be picked up because they still need longer time to continue grow up to increase fruit size and better taste from the trees in order to let any one fruit buyer can feel better taste when they eat this kind of fruit later. If they can buy this kind of fruit to eat later, then this New Zealand farmer's his fruit buyers can buy the best taste of this kind of fruit to eat from an yone supermarket in New Zealand. Consequently, many New Zealand supermarkets will choose to buy any kinds of fruits from this farmer fruit supplier when they feel this farmer's fruits can provide more better taste fruits to compare other farmers' fruits.

Thus, due to New Zealand is one farming main income source country. It's any kinds of fruits and meats need to be export to overseas to sell , instead of local sale. It's GDP percent is very high to whole country 's overall income source. So, any one New Zealand farmer individual and any one farming worker individual working behavior will influence its economy whether it is influenced to grow or recession possible. Moreover, it also seems that farming workers' farming knowledge and skill will influence themselves farming daily activities to achieve the aim of the number of increase or decrease to any kinds of fruits whether they are better taste or the number of increase of decrease to any kinds of meats whether they are better taste to supply to any one New Zealand fruit or meat buyers to eat from any one New Zealand supermarket. So, it implies that any one New Zealand farming worker individual farming behavior may influence any kinds of fruits or any kinds of meat taste because they are transported to any one supermarket to sell in New Zealand.

Consequently, if New Zealans had many farmers can teach god farming knowledge and skill to let their any one farming workers know how to decide judgement to decide when it is right time to pick up any kinds of fruits from trees , or how to grow them on soil in order to let they can grow rapidly. Then, many different kinds of fruits can be provided to let any one New Zealanders can eat the best taste of fruits when their fruits are supplied to any one New Zealand supermarkets. Even, if they knew how to feed foods to pigs, cows, sheeps to eat daily. Then they can be more health and they can provide the best taste of meats to let any one New Zealanders can buy their meats from any one New Zealand supermarkets. Moreover, their fruits and meats can be transported to overseas to let any one country fruits or meats buyers can choose any kinds of New Zealand meats and fruits to buy to eat from themselves countries supermarkets. Then, many overseas fruit and meat buyers will perfer to choose New Zealand any kinds of fruits or meats to buy to compare other countries fruits or meats to buy when they go to any one local supermarkets.

On conclusion, it seems that New Zealand farming workers themselves farming behavior may influence their farming employers any kinds of fruits or meats sale number and income because their farming task behaviors must influence whether their fruits or meats taste are the better taste or worse taste to compare their other local farmers (the farmer competitors) whose fruits or meats taste. If tthe farmer's any one farming worker can be trained to learn how to know to feed animals skill and when is the most right time to pick up any kinds of fruits from trees or how to grow them on the soil methods. Due to these farming worker individual farming behavior may influence his different finds of fruits and meats sale number to be increase or decrease, so these any one New Zealand farmer must need to depend on any one farming worker whose farming working methods, if their farming working behaviors can be the best to influence any kinds of fruits to grow rapid or any kinds of pigs, cows, sheeps animals grow up rapidly , then their sale number may be increase significantly and their taste can be improved to let any New Zealand or overseas meat or fruit buyer to buy to eat to feel from any one New Zealand or overseas supermarkets, then New Zealand's agriculture industry must be influenced to increase. In the world, any one fruit or meat buyer must choose to buy New Zealand's fruit and meat to eat in prefer to compare other countries' fruits and meats. So, New Zealand's GDP may be influenced to raise from any one New Zealand farming worker individual farming working behaviors.

Reasons why human behavior may influence economic recession or growth?

Can ourselves daily behaviors or activies influence ourselves countries' economic growth or recession? I shall attempt to explain the reasons why they have direct or indirect relationship between human behavior and economy growth or recession as below:

I shall indicate environment pollution case to attempt to explain above question. Our societies had been experiencing servious environment pollution challenge. However, environment pollution , such as air pollution is caused by air planes and vehicles emission by air planes and vehicles emission as well as water pollution is caused by plastic rubblish, or dirty water or oil or gas chemical material, these both kinds of pollution ought may bring economic recession and this both kinds of pollution are caused by human ourselves daily foolish activities.

I believe human behavior and economy and pollution which have cause and effect relationship. I shall analyze this environment pollution case to explain why they have case and effect relationship between human foolish behavior and environment pollution and economic recession as below:

When global societies had many people like to buy cars to drive to bring emission to fresh air on the roads as well as many manufacturing factories will bring emission to pollute fresh air in their manufacturing processes. Factories and cars will bring air pollution , due to factories need to pollute fresh air in order to manufacture many products and car owners need to drive their cars to go to offices or leisure places. Their cars will also bring emisson to pollute fresh air. On consequence, car owners themselves frequent driving behaviors and factory workers themselves frequent manufacturing behaviors may bring environment pollution. Technology or human behavior whether may influence economic growth or recession. Moreover, air planes also brings emission to pollute air when they are flying in sky. Also, when ships bring oil pollution or sea plastic rubblishs bring pollution to global oceans.

In fact, manufactuers and cars owners, such as factories workers manufacturing behaviours ans car owners driving behaviors and pilots driving air planes flying behaviors and ships transport behaviors, which may cause plastic rubblish, oil or gas emission to sky or sea or on the road to cause ocean and air pollution is serious. However, human ourselves need to buy cars to drive to satisfy ourselves driving leisure or enjoyment, travelers need to catch air planes to travel to enjoy leisure needs, factories workers need help factories to manufacture many products to sell to customers to satisfy their using needs. oil exploration needs to find lands to explore new oil lands.

All of these business and leisure activites may bring serious air and water pollution. However, due to serious air and water pollution will bring earth warming challenge , such as some countries temperature will be influences to rise up to 40 degree or higher br earth warming. However, earth warming is caused by air and ocean pollution. Pollution must be caused by human ourselves, driving cars leisure and factories manufacturing business activities. Hence, if human decided to continue to do these foolish behaviors, we only pursue to manufacture different kinds of industrial products or drive cars to enjoy leisure aims, but we also neglect ourselves behaviors may bring environment pollution. Then, earth warming or earth temperature will be influenced to rise up absolutely in long term. Moreover, if our future earth will be influenced to bring serious high temperature effect by human ourselves these foolish behaviors.

On consequencey, warth warming will bring serious economic losses in possible because when ourselves earth temperature had been influenced to rise up to 40 degree or high. Ourselves health will be caused poor, due to we will feel difficult breath, we must need often tried and hard to work, due to our nervous and health will be influenced to poor by pollution and earth warming effect. Also, we need to pay more money to see doctors when we had long life. Then, our societies will lose may strong labors to help manufacturers to work, e.g. factories will reduce workers number to help manufacturers to produce more different kinds of products, due to workers health is general poor. Due to lacking enough workers to manufacture products, our societies will begin to reduce enough supply number of products to sell to global consumers to satisfy their use needs.

On conclusion, in behaviroal economic view, our societies will lose many labors due to their bodies are not health by air and water pollution. Global economic and business activities will be influenced to worse by global workers reducing number reason. So, economic recession will begin to occur in possible when pollution reaches the serious level.

CHAPTER FIVE

Explaining How Distance Learning May Increase Students Number

Science and engineering subject educational challenge

USA science and engineering subject future challenge

Nowadays, US played a critical role in establishing leadership in science and engineering (S&E) education aspect, however, the next generation of scientists will need to solve these science and engineering subject educational challenge. For example, how to ensure future generations continue to reap the benefits of fundamental S&E research. They need to give big ideas of what benefits can be given to the next generation students. Such as US country science and engineering research will lose serious and non-value if it doesn't ensure what benefits can be given to the next generation. So, IT educational method can be attempted to solve this science and engineering subject educatonal challenge, due to this subject students need to often to do research and experiment to prepare to finish their assignments. Internet will be one useful tool to help students to gather any science and engineering datas to finish their assignment easily. So, computers and internet must need to be used by students in any school classrooms.

The catalyze interest and investment in fundamental (S&E) research which needs the basis for discovery, invention and innovation benefits. They are meant to define a set of cutting-edge research agendas and processes that are uniquely suited for (S&E)'s broad portfolio of investment and will require collaborations with industry, private foundations, other agencies, science academies and societies and universities.

On US (S&E) student numbers learning difficulty aspect, how to solve some of the most pressing problems the world faces as well as lead to discoveries not yet known to our (S&E) education, such as US development (S&E) education? For example, US is experiencing a period of significant demographic shifts , the Census Bureau projects that by 2050 year, minorities will comprise 53% of the population.

Nowadays, it has approximately 30% of people are now working in (S&E) are minorities. To maintain US leadership in science, the nation must address the challenge of broadening participation for the next generation. So, to solve the one (S&E) student numbers shortage common problem. It will develop scalable ways to educate the potential among traditionally underrepresented groups, including women. African Americans, native Americans, persons with disabilities, people from rural areas and people of low socioeconomic status. Thus, US (S&E) student numbers can be the next generation (S&E) student numbers shortage problem gap or take advantage of new opportunities. US universities will need to teach the uneducated and less computer and internet knowledge African Americans, native Americans, persons with disabilites, people from rural aread and people of low socioeconomic staus science and engineering students how to use internet to gather data from computers to prepare their learning easily in the future.

On US (S&E) teacher teaching challenge aspect, imagine researchers being able to precisely foresee future characteristics of biological organisms, human disease risk, drug therapy response, food crop yields and environmental remediation to name just a few. Nature is full of diverse species in all shapes, colors and sizes. Each with characteristics resulting from a complex interaction of genetics and the environment. For example, the universally recognized biggest gap in biological knowledge is their inability to predict an organism's observable characteristics, its phenotype from what we know about its genetics and environment. Many factors influence the traits in an organism, making this prediction is extreme complex. This biological educational challenge will require research across biology, computer science, mathematics, behavioral sciences and engineering. This initiative understanding the rules of life predicting phenotype will include research in data integration analysis, modeling and informatics techniques. So, US science and engineering teachers need to learn how to apply internet to raise teaching quality to teach their students more easily and effectively and efficiently in classroom.

I recommend an online platform of data tools for large scale analysis of complex biological problems will be one suitable tool to be used for educational aim in the future. I also recommend to apply internet teaching toole to change future school science and engineering experiment work place to carrying on any science and engineering experimenting in school laboratories. It will require a changing future school experiment work force, making (S&E) education and lifelong learning important priorities. We need have a unique opportunity to actively shape the development and use of techniques to improve the quality of experiment work when also increasing productivity and economics growth in manufacturing and in service sectors, such as healthcare and education from internet technology. For example, (S&E) activities rely increasingly on infrastructure that is diverse in space, cost and implementation time , everything from major observatories to nationwide sensor networks to smaller experiments from internet educational tool.

The (S&E) education major challenge is that there many important potential experiments and facilities that fall between these amounts; this gap results in missed opportunities that leave essential science undone. The long term consequences of that neglect will be profound for science as well as for US action's economy, security and competitiveness. So, US universities science and engineering lecturers will need a new approach to research in infrastructure. One more dynamic and flexible internet teaching tool will be in response to this new reality in the future.

The eduational method challenges to higher education engineering lecturers

High education (HE) has become more globalized and is slowly changing from being teacher-centered to study-centered. Industry is ever more demanding of graduates' employability and value. Degree programs are required to address the learning outcomes their graduates should attain (including : discipline and contextual knowledge, practice knowledge and skills and personal and professional attributes).

What challenges to higher education engineering lecturers meet? For example, teaching core engineering concepts to assist student engineers to learn how to apply them to solve a problem sometimes supplemented with placements. This is traditional teaching method challenge, so engineering lecturers need to change to apply technological educational method to let engineering students to feel learning more easily. However, new technological teaching method is popular to be applied to lecturers, but it also encounter difficulty, such as students need to understand e.g. risk, critical thinking, business acumen, social desirability of designs and how to adapt their role in innovation to attract student engineers' attention.

How to meet demand for engineering graduates? High education is growing into engineering qualifications, essential to attractive, creative, enthusiastic, engaged students from all backgrounds. Thus, higher education engineering lecturers are hoped to train engineering students who can have self-directed learning, transferable skills development. So, higher education engineering lecturer role of teacher is as an educator and learning facilitator. For example, engineering education needs apply new technological educational innovation. Innovation in engineering education can ensure transform students into graduates who are well prepared for future engineering practice, exploits new science and technology is responsive to change socio-economic and environmental contexts. Because nowadays, engineers are hoped creative, innovation ready, entrepreneurial, critically thinking , socially responsible engineers.

Thus, higher education engineering lecturers need have innovation mind to arrange how to gather data to prepare each lesson to teach engineering students from internet , such as engineering lecturers disciplinarily with increasing use of problem and project based learning, group learning and assessment, authentic workplace learning and research –based /enquiry learning. It seems future lectures need to own innovation and critically thinking mind. Then, who can train students to own the same mind to learn more easily and independently from internet assistance.

What are the limites to the future of higher educational opportunities for India ?

Nowadays, India's education system is as one of the world's largest, has been studied and reflected on through academic papers, used as a case study and been the subject of many renowned books. This is a traditional India educational models. The educational innovation and change are required and understanding that change will be essential to India education system because India's demographic trend means it will soon over take China as the world's largest population. Thus, India is encountering population growth challenge to cause shortage of school supply to students to study. The Indian higher education system is facing on challenge is being driven by economic and demographic change by 2020 year. India will be the world's third largest economy with a correspondingly rapid growth in the size of its middle classes. Currently , over 50% of India population is under 25 years old by 2020 year . India will outpace China as the country with the largest tertiary age population.

Thus, Indian higher education is facing with four broad challenges, such as:

The supply –demand gap challenge: BY 2020 year, the Indian government aims to achieve 30% gross enrolment, which will mean providing to million university places, an increases of 14 million in six years.

The low quality of teaching and learning challenge: Shortage of faculty , poor quality teaching, outdated curricular, lack of accountability and quality assurance and separation of research and teaching.

Constraints on research and innovation challenge: With a very low level of PHD enrolment. India does not have enough high quality researchers, there are less opportunities for interdisciplinary and multidisciplinary working, lack or early stage research experience, a weak ecosystem for innovation and low levels of industry engagement.

Uneven growth and access to opportunity challenge: Socially access to higher education is uneven with inequalities in enrolment areas population groups and geographies.

Thus, India government needs to reform educational policy, but many predict higher education leader academics and policy makers in India to explore their views on what the future holds for them and link to collaborate with the UK. For example, India educational organizations can co-operate with UK, USA etc. developed countries' famous and successful educational institutes to apply internet to teach India students by distance learning method. If India students had any learning challenges , who can send their questions to enquire these overseas countries' lecturers to get feebacks easily by email channel. Also, India teachers can send email with overseas developed countries' teachers to discuss different teaching methods easily.

Thus, key challenges are facing the system includes educational quality assurance, credit transfer system; between higher education and vocational skills solution method include promoting higher education and vocational skills stream and teacher training in higher education, change college education method to improve the quality of teaching and learning, private educational business sector will continue to grow , but for profit high education is unlikely to be sanctioned soon international cooperating with UK institutions to make the most of educational opportunities and foreign education providers need to take a long term view and build closer multi -dimensional relationship with Indian institutions.

Education challenges of the global science students in 21 St century

The national assessment of educational progress indicated a scale of 1 to 300 for reporting performance in science. Form 1996 year to 2005 year, the national average 4th grade science score increased from 147 to 151 , but there was no measurable change in the 8th grade score, and the 12th grade score actually decreased from 150 in 1996 year to 147 in 2005 year. Digest of education statistics 2010 (pg.2, pg. 63). It brings this question: What factors cause global science students whose scores can not raise in the 8th grade as well as the 12th grade score actually decreases from 1996 to 2005 year in common.

The performance data showed global middle school and high school science students on an average are performing around the 50 percentage. The OECD (2009) program showed that international student assessment evaluates the quality , equity and efficiency of school system in some 70 countries that together, make up nine-tenths of the world economy. Its tests are designed to find out whether science students can use what who have learned in schools and apply their knowledge to real life situations and problems. It's test result show countries where which stand in relation to other countries and how effective which educate their students. Thus, it implies global science students' learning methods and teachers' educational method will have close relationship to influence global science student individual score performance and learning performance. It brings this question: Can technological education method improve science students' learn methods and raise quality of teachers' educational method?

However, global science students will feel challenges to learn science. The reasons include, such as an individual learning level, because of an increasingly learning world learning competition will influence overseas university student enrollment or even from across the student himself/ herself country but from across the world. As a society, if it's universities or secondary schools are not able to develop a next generation that is capable of solving the pressing problems of human will face in many areas, including climate change, social and economic inequality and dwindling natural and energy resources. It is therefore difficult to figure not now schools can address the issue of how to evaluate the performance of our science students.

I recommend how to apply internet educational method to solve these challenges, such as:

The first method is that global science teachers, parents and country leaders in different countries government, business and academic need to consider how earth science challenges, such as global climate changing, food shortage, water and air pollution etc. problems, due to globalization and advances in technology influence. So, they can apply internet to encourage science students to know how these above natural disasters causes from online learning. So, online learning method can influence science students to consider these earth warming result to raise their interest to be proficient in creativity, critical , thinking and communication of ability to achieve their best learning performance in possible in the future.

The second method is that I think we can meet objective by designing a online learning environment around networked learning technologies , a project based learning approach and online and science student in person real natural environment traveling method with school science teachers together on Saturday and Sunday non-school days. Before science students can find or gather any natural science related data to prepare to assist whose studying more easily out classrooms from internet , then their science teachers can bring them to visit natural environment, such as natural parks or forests to investigate different plants, animals and natural lands themselves to learn more easily as well as their visiting the country real natural environment both, the science teachers can let science students to absorb what the actual natural challenges are actually occurring. Thus, science students need to gather data and learn how these natural disaster causes from internet learning methods, due to interent learning method will raise many global science student individual interest to learn science subject in short time effectively.

The trend of challenges of educational development of the 21st century global society

The 21st century educational skills became known as critical thinking, communication, collaboration and creativity. So, every individual student is needed own ability to solve any learning challenges. In the global manufacturing economies that existed 50 years ago, students need own reading, writing and calculation ability to learn easily, even how to gather useful data to prepare to study from internet channel. Because, in modern world, students must be proficient communicators, creators, critical thinkers and collaborators and students need have effort to study these subject areas, including foreign languages, the arts, geography, science, law, business and social studies etc. subjects. It seems internet channel is the sole learning method to let any subject students to gather data to prepare their learning more easily in the short time.

As the same time, due to workforce skills and demands have changed dramatically in the last twenty years, e.g. many labor manufacturing method had change to new technological manufacturing method., even, labor service job will also change to artificical intelligence service job as soon as possible. Moreover, global employers need to employ employees who need have a rapid increase in jobs involving non-routine, analytic and interactive communication skills. Thus, it causes today's job market requires competencies , such as critical thinking and the ability to interact with the company employees from many different cultural backgrounds employee working environment. Thus, students need own these critical thinking and excellent communication skills to prepare to work in society. It seems any country's schools need to teach students these skills to prepare to work in societies. It brings this question: Can internet channel attract students to learn how to use critical thinking mind and attitude to solve their learning difficulty and future working difficulty in any working environment easily?

To answer this question, we need to know what the critical thinking is. Critical thinking and problem solving can be defined as: Using various types of reasoning (inductive, deductive etc.) as appropriate to the situation , using systems thinking to analyze how parts of a whole interact with each other to produce overall outcomes in complex systems; making judgements and decisions in effectively analyzed and evaluated evidence, arguments, claims and belief, analyzing and evaluating major alternative points of view, synthesizing and making connections between information and arguments, interpreting information and drawing conclusion based on the best analysis, reflecting critically on learning experiences of unfamiliar problems in both conventional and innovative ways and identifying and asking significant questions that clarifying various points of view and leading to better solutions (Catalina Foothills School District). Thus, if the university student owned these abilities to learn. I believe that who must feel not difficulties to learn.

Then, it brings this question: How critical thinking and problem solving can be integrated into classroom teaching and learning across a variety of grade levels and disciplines. For art subject student example, music students individually articulate different ways to interpret the same musical passage. Students then compare the various interpretations and determine which one is most effective, taking into account age-appropriate considerations, such as the style of the music. For another world languages student example , with the job title omitted , students read various job/career advertisements and then match the appropriate job title to the ad. Students are divided into groups. Each group is asked to investigate 3 to 5 different career/job sites and identify the jobs and careers that are in high demand in a particular city, region or country. Then, students can present their findings of the most suitable world languages learning method to the class. Next, for science students example, who need to research how the physical and chemical properties of different natural and human designed materials affect their decomposition under various conditions. So, I recommend students can apply internet to gather data to compare their findings to the material evidence used by scientists to reconstruct the lives of past cultures, as well as create a map of their classroom as a future written descriptions of artifacts and what who imply about the cultures, discovered by scientists. So, the science students can be trained to learn how to apply critical thinking to plan and conduct scientific investigations and write detailed explanations based on their evidence when they often apply internet to gather data to compare their findings to the material evidence used by scientists to make judgement to prepare their learning in every lesson.

Thus, the owned critical thinking skillful science students who can compare their explanations to those made by scientists and relate them to their own understandings of the natural and designed world more easily. Finally for social studies students example, in groups , students explore how selected societies for fuel (e.g. England's use of its forests at the beginning of the industrial revolution) and the economic impact of that use. The owned critical thinking skillful social studies students will choose to use videoconference by internet oral communication channel (e.g. www.skp.com) to collect information from relevant government officials about the use of corn for biofuel instead of food and analyze the environmental and economic implications of this use. For example, after they gather data to find any scientific evidences from internet channel. Then, they can choose to use sound reasoning and relevant scientific evidence examples, who can also analyze the historical evolution of a contemporary public policy issue, place it within a cultural and historical context, and use a online digital publishing tool to report the work from internet channel. In conclusion, above of these learning behaviors, which are the owned critical thinking or skillful students who will choose to decide to do these learning behaviors habitually from internet channel. Also, I feel global schools specially, universities and secondary schools ought train whose students to learn how to use internet channel to gather data to do critical thinking to solve any learning problems easily.

Future science, technology, engineering and mathematics students' learning challenges

Science, technology, engineering and mathematics will be popular subjects to any developed countries, such as US, UK, Japan as well as developing countries, such as China, India, Hong Kong, Korea growth subjects, even global economic competitiveness and the demand of these subject students will increase to study these subjects in US, even global. Because global many employers will increase demand these qualified workers, due to these qualified workers will have shortage of numbers to supply to global employment market. It trends in k-12 and higher education science and math. Also, preparation coupled with demographic and labor supply trends point to a serious quality of educational worker challenge. Such as, global nations need to increase the supply and quality of knowledge workers whose specialized skills to enable them to work productivity within technology industries and occupations in global. It will bring this question: Can internet technology can raise these Science, technology, engineering and mathematics subjects of teachers' quality of teaching level?

Nowadays, US Department of labor already investing about $14 billion one year in the nation's workforce system and in increasing the science, technology, engineering and math. students' skills and education. So, how to raise student's individual skills to US competitiveness and growth to science, technology , engineering and math. subjects that will be US educational development challenge. Opinion leaders and the publish board agree that education in math. and science is critical to the nation's future success. According to a recent educational testing service survey, it indicated 61% of opinion leaders and 40% of the general publish identify math, science, and technology skills will be the most important ingredients in the nation's strategy to compete in the global economy (Zinth 2006).

Thus, in US , the science, technology, engineering and math. students' multi-faceted education and workforce challenge include: Many students never feel studying these subjects easily, because of inadequate preparation in math. and science or poor teacher quality in their K-12 education systems(ACT 2006). Many who are academically qualified for postsecondary studies in science and math. fields of both the two and four year levels don't pursue those programs. The might be dissuaded by disappointing curricula and course of study, relatively low salary in these professional (American Association Of State College And Universities 2005).

In conclusion, it is the right time US , even global science, technology, engineering and math. subjects teachers can attempt to learn how to apply internet to teach their students in classroom to let them to feel to learn these subjects effectively and easily.

Future trends in K-12 education challenges

In the future, the majority of trends in K-12 education will use technology , such as cloud computing, mobile learning, learning analytics, open content, remote or virtual laboratories are directly related to improved student learning. However, it will have difficulty to achieve technology education to k-12. Because these young students need time to learn how to apply different computer software or high technology equipment to learn. Moreover, the changing uses of technology require that teachers also change their methods of instruction.

Online cloud computing, mobile learning , virtual laboratories, learning analytics, open content and remote technological learning methods which aim to achieve the studying or learning plan to encourage students can direct their own learning. As a result, teachers must shift from being holders and distributors of knowledge to becoming instructional facilitators who encourage students to direct their own learning.

Thus, the challenges of technological education will need to achieve how to direct students feel easy to use technological tools to learn conveniently. Several tools are available to support teachers. Such as social learning networks, e-portfolios and cloud computing allow teachers virtually connect and encourage discussion about best practice among teachers. For cloud computing education tool example, it comprises internet-based tools that don't live on an individual device. This flexibility allow for access to materials stored and the cloud at any location. Students can access homework assignments, readings and support materials anywhere, who can connect with the cloud.

Commonly used examples of cloud computing sharing devices are drop box and google drive. Also, cloud computing is popular in distance learning programs for obvious reasons. There are three categories of cloud computing that may be useful to k-12 educators (Nagel, D. 2013) indicated it includes infrastructure -as-a-service (i.e. virtualization). This category describes scalable virtual machines, bandwidth and storage capacities, platform-as-a-service (Pass). This category describes the environment in which the development and delivery of applications occurs and software-as-a-service (psas). This category describes software that is created for a specific organization's unique needs. Thus, k-12 students need to spend time to learn what are these category difference, then who can choose to use what may or method to use cloud computing to learn more easily in four years.

So, it brings this question: Why k-12 students need to apply cloud computing to learn. The reason is mobile technologies have also attracted the attention of high profile educational publishers, such as person, e-books, e-magazines publishers and interactive textbook have optimized for mobile platforms and devices and can easily replace heavier traditional textbooks. It also allow children to interact with material using simple fingers swipes and pinches, which eliminates the need for detailed instructions. It seems it has one day detailed instructions and electronic books will be popular to let any young students to accept to study, such as primary and high school and university students who can learn from computers or mobiles in future one day. Thus, it is the right time k-12 students to learn how to apply technology to learn.

Anyway, distance or distributed e-learning education is one of the most complex issues facing higher education institutions today. However, there are much challenge to education k-12 students by learning. How can teachers teach k-12students by distance education, e-learning or distributed learning method to achieve the effective learn outcome? Is it an extensive of the k-12 classroom or replacement leave? Distance learning is a subject of distributed learning, focusing on k-12 students who may be separated in time and space from their pears and the instructor. Distributed learning can occur either on or off campus, providing k-12 students with greater flexibility and eliminating time as a barrier to learning, campus or online.

There are many implications of technology into education , i.e. in making learning distributed . So, the challenge indicates k-12 students to learn how to allocate time to learn from distance learning technology method. For example, eating time, sleeping time, doing homework time and learning time allocation. Teachers need teach students how to arrange and allocate time to learn or sleep or do homwork effectively and easily.

Distance learning online education challenges

Common assumptions about higher education include: schools know the student profile and learner preferences for learning and service delivery, student credit hours and full time equivalents are relevant units of measure in distributed education, completion of the curriculum is the measure of competency, traditional institutional models (e.g. for classroom instruction, governance and financing) will be successful in an e-learning educational method, higher education must provide all components of the educational process (e.g. content, curriculum, services and credentialing), external providers of educational services (e.g. courses or tutoring from an internet start-up) are bad or of lower quality than educational institutions, quality is better in a not-for-profit educational organization than in a for profit one, high education will be driven out low quality from bad online education influence, distributed learning is a variable option for all post-secondary education institutions, the faculty member is the focal point od the learning process.

So,All higher education institutions must develop their own distributed learning programs. Although, these assumptions characteristic are good, but which may not all apply to distance distributed learning. Some educational organizations have either inadequate or inappropriate for distributed learning. For example, the nation of credit for seat time has sustained current model of higher education, but will it suffice for a future represented by distributed learning?

However, technological education will bring these negative influences to students. What are the challenges in influence students psychology from information age mind set? When students often use computer or laptop to learning , constant connectivity, they will reduce time to communicate or make close relationship with whose friends and family at any time and from any place. Then, every online learning student behavior and value will be influences, such as: computers aren't technology only. It is whose part of life, the internet is better than TV reality is no longer real, doing is more important than knowing, trial-and-error, experimentation is preferable to logic , multitasking is a way of life, typing is preferable to handwriting, staying online learning connected is essential every day.

There is zero tolerance for online on-line learning time delays. Thus, the way, schools must organize their educational institutions to change educational method to achieve online learning time and private entertainment time to be balances to every student. Although, online education can give convenient and fast speed to gather information benefits to young students to study. But, educators need to consider these online education challenges which, online educational students will encounter , such as : What kind of support to faculty needs to develop engaging and empowering online environment? Are educators using the unique capabilities of the web to make learning environments engaging and effective? Do educators know which students will learn best of a distance and those for whom it is a poor choice? Thus, it brings this question: Does distributed learning support a specific strategic goal for the educational institutions or is the rationale?

To gain the commitment of all those who must support a major initiative (board , executive cabinet, faculty, teaching staff etc.) , it is important to articulate clearly the strategic goals behind the institution's interest in distributed learning. For example, which is the institution's commitment to educational access? Would distributed education enhance the fulfilment of that goal? Will it seem inconsistent with policies on selectivity and/or the importance of the residential experience? Does distributed education complement educational institution's mission, culture and historic strengths? Do the institutions have clear rationale for distributed eduaction?

Corporate learners work for corporations and are seeking education to maintain or the employing corporation and not by the individual acting alone. Professional enhancement learners are seeking to advance careers or shift careers. They are working adults who make the educational purchasing decision on their own. Degree-completion adult learners are working to complete a degree at an older age . They frequently are working adults who must balance work and family needs with their educational goals. College experience learners are preparing for life , e.g. the traditional students. This segment includes many of the 18 to 24 year old residential college students for whom the coming age process is almost as important as academic achievement. Finally, I shall suggest pre-college (k-12) learners are interested in doing degree level work prior to the completion of high school. This learner age segment may be interested and is more acceptable in getting studying to compare other learnerage segment from internet learning channel.

Developing countries educational challenges
Future challenges influence high education
development in long term
Nowadays, developing countries, such as
India, China, Korea, Thailand, Hong Kong etc. are facing educational challenges. I feel developing countries governments have responsibilities to consider every citizens who can have effort to study or learn in themselves countries fairly. How to achieve the politician education is seen as a solution to poverty , social mobility, equality of opportunity, social problems, management of the changes in values educational systems, the key productivity and human resource development in primary, secondary and tertiary different student learning stages of educational aspects.
To the developing countries teachers, education is seen as that which should contribute to the development of the potential of the child to contribute to the development of the nation and by extension " world development". The development countries can't provide excellent education quality and quantity to students . They have these similar characteristics to influence to develop their education : relatively small population , small land area, limited natural resources, range of diversity , high level of dependency on international forces, economic challenges. Thus, I feel they need education reform, the perceptions of the important of education and the limitations are faced by both terms of quality and quantity has resulted on reduction reform. Education reform means the implication of globalization methods . It necessary to reform their education systems for it requires them to adapt their own education content to meet not only their local demands, but also their international concerns.

These developing countries educational major challenges, include these aspects mainly: on economic aspect, under educational level youth unemployment, skill shortages in key areas of the economy, new jobs associated with higher technology occupations requiring higher entry levels, a mismatch between the graduates and the available jobs. On social aspect, the non-educational students spend waste time to do bad behaviors to influence whose relationships between families or teachers in societies. Doing bad behaviors , such as illegal international drug trade, high crime rate and gang warfare, HIV/AIDS disease increasingly the case of death rate for those between the age of 15 and 45 years the largest crime age group.

Thus, developing country governments need how to solve these challenges. On changing environment aspect, it concerns on the nature and organization of work, the need for retraining and retooling , the important role of knowledge or a factor of production, the emphasis on information technology. On political aspect, it concerns on a democracy, peace, a creation of a state of esteem society.

In general, these development have these major challenges on education aspect: Existing curriculum content and pedagogical methods are being questioned. Students leave school ill-prepared for the world of work and adulthood, high incidence of illiteracy and numeracy, marked gender differences in achievement, curriculum changes without the necessary changes in assessment, untrained teachers at the early childhood, primary and secondary levels. Student under-performance , high levels of student attrition, student repetition of grade levels, harmonization of curriculum and assessment across the region , inadequate policy for recruitment and selection of teachers, lack of systems of certification evaluation and licensing of teachers, unsure about eh place of tech/voc. In secondary schools, the harmonization of competencies, skills for certification of students for the world of work.

To conclude, any developing countries major educational challenges have these characteristics: there seems to be no other alternative right now and in the near future for them, but to collaborate in all areas of development utilizing the new technologies and benefiting from those that have begun the change process at the same time, maximizing the resources at their immediate disposal.

The question demonstrates how universities have responded the pressures created by the country's economic recession. For example, universities in the UK are already being seriously affected by the short term impact of both economic recession and the crisis in public finances.

The more substantial reductions in expenditure now awaited are likely to increase the existing planned cuts to create major existing challenges to which the sector must respond. The UK economic recession and the public funding crisis are closely related, but which are not the same. However, UK universities have been facing some short term challenges, such as changes in student choices and graduate employment, due to consequences of economic recession in UK. Because it can influence UK students feel lack confidence about how the subjects that students wish to study and the kind of employment who find on leaving higher education in the future. Thus, it has close relationship between the UK economy changes in the post-recession world, as well as with the changes in student support and graduate contribution.

How other governments and other higher education systems have responded to economic recession in the short term. I suggest governments need to concern why economic recession had caused , it is as part of a long term strategy to build intellectual capital (knowledge economy). Increasing investment in higher education significant increases in funding for research, a stabilization of the per capita teaching grant and the introduction of higher and deferred fees for undergraduates. Engaging with business in knowledge transfer, skills and internships to universities to promote what subject(s) will be the most popular and successful teaching subject(s) in the univeristy and explaining the reasons why these subjects can attract students to study from internet knowledge exchange channel. These internet teaching promoting method will be possible to solve economic challenges to influence global students to make university choice to study more easily.

Future challenges India and China medical education

China and India is the most populated geographical area of the world (1.2 billion in India). Thus, medical service will be much demanded in India. However, China and India have the largest number of medical challenges, but they can't provide excellent quality health care to patients. Why such a situation has arisen in India and China? The problem is the clinical settings where doctors avail training.

In recent years, technology and health care systems have profound changes. To cope with these changes , medical educational institutions around the world have been increasingly confronted with the challenge of making their curricula more meaningful and relevant to the needs of the community. So, apply technology method to learn medical education and suggested strategies for direction is needed to adopt the medical education changes.

For example, many medical schools have now translated into all major languages, has been very widely adopted as basis for reform of medical education. So, India and China medical lecturers can teach their mother language to compare English teaching to let medical students to understand what their teaching more easily. Many of the medical schools in Asia have traditional teacher –centered and hospital based training with a few exceptions only. Medical teachers , planners and policy makers are to be well-informed of such trends and utilize these in planning, implementing and evaluating medical training programs to increase relevance and quality and to produce need-based human resources for health for the regions, such as India and China. So, internet will be the best language learning method for these medical lecturers and students.

What medical problem to Indian and Chinese face? Indian and Chinese get a significant number of medical tourists, a reflection of the high level of medical expertize that Indian and Chinese patients possess . However, a majority of India and China citizens have limited assess to quality health care, less than half of Indian and Chinese children are fully immunized. Similarly, the minimum of three checkups during pregnancy remains unavailable for half of Indian and Chinese pregnant women. India and China universities are just degree selling shops. Medical schools should make changes in the curriculum, adopt innovate strategies for enhancing students' learning improve the methods used to assess students' performance and focus on the professional development of faculty as teachers and educators.

In China and India , medical students follow a rote method of learning, so the clinical bedside knowledge is far below the requirement . How is this going to make India and China reliable doctors? In conclusion, medical education is a professional subject. So, China and India need concern how well to train doctors' skills to prepare to provide excellent medical service to their patients to achieve health satisfactory level to every hospitals. Online/ distance learning learning channel will be one good method to let medical students to learn when they live so far distance to their university in India or China.

Reference
ACT 2006. Developing the STEM education pipleing
IOWA city IA: ACT.
American Association Of State College And Universities,
2005. " Strengthening the science and math. pipeline for a better American policy matters vol. 2, number 11 . Nov. /Dec.

Critical thinking rubric created by the Catalina Foothills School District, http://rubrics.metiri, wikispaces.net/file/view/ Calalina_Foothills_Critical_Thinking_Rubric_1.doc

Digest Of Education Statistics 1020. Retrieved from http://nces.edu.gov/pubsearch/pubsinfo.asp?pubid=2011015

OCED program for international assessments (PISA) 2009 results. Retrieved from http:// www.oecd. org/edu/pisa/2009.

Nagel, D. " Cloud computer to make up 35% of k-12 budgets in 4 years." IT trends research, The Journal February 19, 2013. http://the journals.com/ articles/201302/19/cloud-computing-to-make-up-35-of-k12-it-budgets

Zinth, Kyle, 2006 Recent State STEM Initiatives. Denver: Education Commission to the states.

Choosing university to study challenge

University campus location choice challenge.

Whether University location can be a competitive advantage to attract students to study? The school (university) location means that the proximity of city center and the proximity of students home. To increase the occupancy rate, the university location is needed to provide as a model and resources based view which will be used to explain why the school location is a kind of competitive advantage for universities. According to Porter theory, it is a part of factor, which has some advantages against the treat of entry. It can decrease the treatment of rivalry. However, a good place has a certainly positive effect for attracting staff and more students. For resource-based view, the location is one of the internal resources. It can be accepted as one of the physical and tangible resource of a university.

I shall apply the first attractive factor of Porter five forces and resource based model to analyze my opinion to explain why school (university location) can influence students to choose the university to study. This view is represented by the opportunities and the threats. The university of thought is the resource based view which is represented by the strengths and weaknesses of the firm. Porter's five force model of competition elements include threats of entrants or substitutes, bargaining power of buyers or suppliers and competition rivalry. A firm's resources include brand name, in-house knowledge of technology, employment of skilled personnel, trade contract, machinery, efficient procedures and capital etc. Such as, both tangible and intangible assets are considered a firm's resources. For a university, customers can be thought as a students, suppliers can be thought as staff. In higher education industry, the good transportation infrastructure and well-connected universities have some advantages against the treat of entry to attract good staff and more students. The place of a university can decrease of treatment of rival and a good place has certainty positive location is an opportunity for universities to attract the students.

The resource based theory of university location competitive advantage challenge

According to the Porter's theory, the resource based theory can apply competitive resources to be identifies to higher education institutions. For higher education institutions, such as resources might include the reputation of certain departments, the grouping together of areas of specialist expertise and the development of technical patents etc. Also higher education resources may not be imperfectly mobile, as the competitive resources of a university identifies tangible, intangible and organizational assets. So, the tangible resources might include campus location, building capacity, conference facilities and medical research facilities. Intangible resources generally include such items as patents, teaching and research performance, service levels and technology and the geographical location of a service. In a university, such intangible resources might include some of the above and may also include employees/ associates, e.g. experienced professors, renowned authors and distinguished teachers. Also, the location of a university can be accepted as physical and tangible resources of a university. However, I believe location is shown as an important factor to affect the students' university enrolment selection decisions.

To sources of competitive advantages are thought to be the reputation of the institution, the curriculum and educational standards, school fees (tuition), location and student activities etc. different factors. Moreover, any university's general client segments include such as, high school graduates, elderly students and international students, that have been influenced by several factors when selecting the best university to study. One of these factors is again location, the proximity to home and easy transportation is critical factor in selecting a university. Presumably, institutions that are located along well-established public transit routes have a competitive advantage over those with poor transit links. Due to the efficiency of innovation activity increased in easily accessible locations with a high density of economic activity. The existence of education and research institutions as well as easily available information is suggested as a reason for this increase. Also private higher education institutions desire to benefit from these flows by locating itself nearby. Therefore, together with other factors, such as existing capital global flows should be existing capital and population, level of income and location decisions of foundation universities. The location, social life campus, proximity of campus to the city center, exchange programs, the curricula infrastructure, languages medium of instruction and activities are the most significant factors to influence students to choose which university to study. By the past statistic indicated that the location has 94% rate, the proximity of campus to the city center has 84% rate. So, it seems the proximity of campus to the city center factor is more prior choice to compare with the school location is close to the student home factor.

Huang (2012) stated that " the right location attracts more students and ensures the revenues of the institution. The location of an educational institution might influence its future prospect of growth. A good location attracts not only more students, but also excellent teaching staff". Because of job opportunities areas, the students are able to get a part-time job and earn extra money for their tuition (Huang, 2012). Marketing concept has four "P", it can apply to university educational business, such as educational promotion, tuition price, teachers of people and school campus location of place.

Finally, I shall give two assumptions to explain why if the university location is not popular to be accepted to the country's students in general, then it will cause who won't choose to study the university. However, even if the university's tuition is reasonable or cheaper or lecturers are famous or reputation or educational advertisement is attractive. In fact, the poor location factor will influence many local or overseas students who don't choose to study the university in the country. The first assumption is that most of students feel that the proximity of the university to the city center factor affects their university final choice decision and the another assumption is that most of students feel that the proximity of university to home affects their university final choice decision. There two assumptions are used to determine the importance of university location to attract the students. In Porter theory, either proximity of city center and/or proximity of student's home of a university factors have same advantages against the treat of entry. It can decrease the treatment of rival and a good place has certainly positive effect to attract teaching staff and more students.

In resource based view, the location can be accepted a kind of internal resources. It can be accepted as one of the sustainable competitive advantages literature, location is a kind of advantage for higher education institutions.

Alternative modes of course delivery chanllenge

The factor of student demand for alternative modes of course delivery is another factor to influence the student who chooses the university to study. Any university's educational program includes program design, material production (both print and e-version), promotion, essay competition, school networks, budgeting, coordinating with various constructors, data base management and program evaluation etc.

Nowadays, university teaching methods may include face-to face, online and hybrid modes of course delivery. However, the several ways to students to deliver their course works ,such as full time, part time, internal/ non campus, external studies/distance education, summer school, winter school, semester study and trimester study. The multi site of a university , e.g. major provider of distance online education operates popular affordable learning for student to use internet to study. Although, students do not need to attend to university classroom to listen lecturer's teaching, but it can reduce face-to-face contact between lecturers and students in university classroom often.

Although, it is a technological and innovative and effective learning modalities. In fact, such new technological teaching modalities may be necessitated to the graduated or master degree or doctoral degree students. But, I feel the online teaching method is not suitable to the bachelor degree students. As the delivery of course content or the commoditization of knowledge must be re-thought to the bachelor's if the student can't enquire whose lecturer any questions to give feedback by face-to-face. Then, who will concern the course to feel more difficult possibly if who can't listen whose lecturer's opinion to solve whose challenges about the course any questions immediately in classroom often.

The second attractive factor of student demand for alternative modes of course delivery is another factor to influence the student who chooses the university to study. Nowadays, university teaching method include face to face, online and hybrid modes of course delivery. However, the several ways to students to deliver their coursework, such as full time, part time, internal/on campus, external studies/distance education, "summer school, winter school, semester study and trimester study." The multi site of a university, e.g. major popular provider of distance online education operates a flexible learning for student to use internet to study. It can reduce face to face contact between teachers and students into university classrooms. Although, it is a technological and innovative and effective learning modalities. In fact, such new technological teaching modalities may be necessitated to the graduated students or master degree or doctoral degree students. But, I feel the online teaching method is not suitable to the bachelor degree students. As the delivery of course content or the commoditization of knowledge must be re-thought to the bachelor degree students because whose knowledge level is limited if the student can't ask whose lecturer any questions by face to face contact. So, students will feel difficult to learn if who can't listen whose lecturers' teaching and to enquire any questions and to give feedback in classrooms immediately. It is possible that who will wait long time to ask many questions to prepare to wait lecturers to give feedback by email later if their lecturers use online teaching method. So it is essential that educators and administrators need to understand differentiated teaching demand to different knowledge level of students. Because student preferences may vary by age, cultural, background, degree types, learning style and matter etc. factors to decide whether whose students are suitable to teach by either online distance learning method between individual student and whose computer or face to face learning method between students and the lecturer in classroom face to face oral teaching educational method. In fact, working adults remain strongly associated either interest in online delivery. However, the availability of evening/weekend choices is the second most important enrollment factor to adult students, due to who consider when enrolling in an institution to indicate the important of face-to-face traditional delivery at not convenient times. So, online education is most clearly suited to independent learners those individuals who are self-motivated and self reliant and those who have a problem solving orientation.

The 2006 year Education Inventions survey found that students interested in associate, bachelor's and master's degrees were most open to whole online delivery, although who were also open to campus-based delivery. Similarly, Gartner's 2008 year e-learning survey found that complete graduate programs offered online continue online. For example, international student demand for Australian higher education is expected to exceed supply in 2020 year, and key 2025 year there will be a shortfall of 22,692 international places on projected demand of 290,848. There numbers imply that to meet demand, Australian universities may want to invest further in online degree/delivery options. However, recent statistics indicate dealing interest in fully online programs in South East Asia, and a survey of 469 transnational students in 2007 year found that a majority of students opposed online provision. These findings suggest that, when branch campuses are found to be prohibitively expensive, the future of transnational programs is in programs that include face-to-face interaction facilitated by an offshore partner of the educational provider. However, education consumers prefer to combine online delivery and geographical proximity. Some of students who are living close to university campus. So who can access to courses delivered in a traditional mode, but chose to take online courses for the flexibility to it afforded them. This is an increasing trend in U.S. institutions as well, whereas online courses are used to cater solely to non-traditional students at a long distance from the campus, increasingly such classes are made available to the mainstream student constituency.

Online and hybrid courses teaching challenge

How can the technology online teaching contributing improve student outcome? At least, learning outcomes for students in online and hybrid courses match those of students in traditional settings. When these are reasons to believe that the hybrid model would produce more effective learning outcomes than the fully-online model in theory. Also evidence suggests that e-learning continues to grow in popularity with the number of hybrid or blended courses increasing at the fastest rate, although online/ hybrid courses certainly do not outcomes courses presented the traditional (i.e. face-to-face traditional classroom) delivery method. These facts help to demonstrate that despite the popularity and increased availability of online courses. However, students still value traditional classroom methods and that online options may not significantly detract from on-campus enrollments.

Hybrid degree programs, also known as blended programs are courses of study that combine traditional classroom based instruction with significant amounts of online instruction, with each passing semester, hybrid degree programs become increasingly popular for students and universities alike. Such courses allow students to reduce time-consuming trips to campus when still benefiting from face-to-face teaching method allow colleges and universities to more effectively use classroom space and to reduce cost. For these reasons, hybrid courses are often praised as the best of both classroom and online teaching methods, it is possible that students have chance to go to classroom to listen lecturer's teaching and who also have chance to use internet to learn from online teaching method as the same time. These is no standard model for hybrid education. Some programs may have students split their time evenly between online and on-campus instruction; some may have students complete the majority of their work online with occasional intensive weekends of on-campus activity and some require students to enroll in a combination of traditional classes as well as strictly online classes. Nowadays, a major educational consulting group found that hybrid or blended learning was the most rapidly growing delivery option when online, hybrid and traditional delivery options were taken into acount. Because of the trend towards more hybrid programming, university officials concern on their potential impact on enrollment levels for on-campus degree programs. Some speculate that hybrid programs have the potential to overtake traditional programs, when others hope to use hybrid programs as stepping stones to attract more students to campus on a full time basis. The structures of different programs reflect institutions' intent to use hybrid programs to attract students from non-traditional areas. For example, Michigam State university's Master of social work hybrid program accepts roughly 25 students per year. In 2008 year, these students lived anywhere from 85 to 435 miles from the main campus, therefore frequent in person activities were not feasible. Gather in addition to completing online assignments, students attended a one-week-summer institute on campus in June and face-to-face instruction sessions in smaller groups organized by geography once per month during the fall and spring semesters. In short, hybrid programs do not necessarily replace on-campus offerings, nor do they commonly draw more students to campus on a full time basis. Rather, they complement existing program offerings by reaching out to new packets of students who have the mean to visit campus on occasion but not regularly.

In conclusion, any university ought follow its subjects, student age, school location and tuition, lecturers' reputation and school research facilities etc. factors to decide whether the course is suitable to be chose either online teaching or face-to-face traditional classroom teaching or hybrid (online and face-to-face both) teaching method to teach whose different degree level students. Because these factors will influence who to choose which kind of subjects to study. For example, if many first year students feel the subjects are difficult to learn. It implies that online distance teaching or hybrid teaching method is not suitable to be taught to them. The traditional face-to-face contact traditional classroom teaching method is more suitable to be taught to them. So, it is flexible to any one of these teaching method to choose to teach any subjects to university student. It is no absolute suitable teaching method to teach any one of subject in any one of university. Because any university is independent, it means that the teaching method is suitable to be taught to the students in the university. It doesn't mean that the same teaching method is suitable to be taught to the students to another university because every university's lecturer's reputation, school tuition fee, course's contents and qualities and student age segment and location is different among of them. It is very difficult to ensure which kind of teaching method must be suitable to be taught to the subject to all universities in any countries.

Choosing university to study challenge

University campus location choice challenge.

The resource based theory of university location competitive advantage challenge

The third attractive factor is concerned how to manage student experience in university life. It is as the totality of a student's interaction with institution. How university management decisions on operational matters are affecting the student individual experience to attract who to study, rather than on teaching and learning activities. University learning experience can decide into those components: the application experience; covering the interactions between potential student and the institutions, up to the point of arrival; the academic experience; students' interactions with the institution associated with their studies, excluding for these purposes teaching and learning processes; the campus experience. Because student life not directly connected with study, which may include activities away from the actual campus and the graduate experience. However, any university's role ought to assist students' transition to employment, instead of education aim.

I shall explain whether this university life experience factors will influence student individual university enrolment choice to study. The management of the student experience is in institutional terms at the heart of responses to their new radically uncertain environment, the externally-driven changes have led to significant new university experience changes in the university structures, policies and processes, resulting in changed institutional cultures. These changes have occurred in different ways depending on the type of university. The research questions that are: Are changes in the higher education leading to change institutional types? Which managerial approaches appear to be the most effective in leading to enhance student experiences and why?

In general, centralizing services, standard
in procedures and strengthening management controls trend to remove discretion at departmental level in the managing experience university. For example, large university can seek to use existing institutional cultures to encourage greater concern for students' needs on the part of both academic and professional staffs. Although, organizational change will happen, it usually will take the form of changing the reporting lines of student related services to create more coherent functional groupings, rather than comprehensive reorganizations. However, a cultural shift in the direction of improving the student experience, in several dimensions regardless of institutional types.

Similarly, whether the university can provide well recruitment service for graduates, this factors can improve the competitive positions in the terms of graduated student recruitment service experience. The cultural shift includes an increased emphasis on employability, new emphasis includes employment-related curriculum changes and enhanced support for recruitment advice and placements, it is concerned to achieve good results for graduated student employment. There is a sense that is focused in response. In believe to student demands on immediate employment rather than on longer term career possibilities. Also, competitive pressure and the consequential need to enhance the support given to student life have led to the introduction of measures to enhance the attractiveness and utility of campuses in various ways. These often utility of campuses in various ways. These often involve library/learning resources improvements, with extended hours of access and the creation of social learning spaces.

However, the different institutional responses to the changing environment that can be detected support the view whether that ideas of effectiveness to institutionally determined. Whether the student university experience can influence who chooses to study the university. So, I shall indicate these research questions, such as: Are changes in higher education leading to changes institutional policies and practices which affect the student experience? Are there differences according to institutional types? Which managerial approaches appear to be the most effective in leading to enhance student experiences and why?

It is important to acknowledge that each student's set of experiences with be unique to that person. However, institutionally intended patterns of the student experience , in areas over which institutions can have some influence. The experience is concerned on student (non-learning) experience. the experiences of student has different respects, mostly in terms of teaching and learning for the particular classes of students (part time, mature, international students). For example, student journey experience can have these elements: First contact and admission, pre-arrival, arrival and orientation, induction, reorientation and reintroduction to study for continuing students and induction preparing to leave, graduation and beyond. Students need to feel satisfaction when who enroll to the university at the first day. The matters, who will contact on the university orientation day. Such as travel to the university accesses to facilities (libraries, computing, student support, teaching and learning, social life and self-development and finance). Because student expectations are variable and unpredictable and because it is not obvious that students are always the best judges of whatever is defined as quality, particularly were academic judgement is involved.

However, the university customer (student satisfaction) vs quality argument is in a traditional relationship. For example, the university service quality includes libraries and IT (information technology) facilities which are closely associated will teaching and learning activities and where academic priorities tend to be bound up with institutional requirement about efficiency and effectiveness. Other university services, such as catering and accommodation are operated on what might be considered to be supplied and demand based commercial principles: Students are indeed the customers of these services. Other student facing services, such as admissions academic administration , student advice and support and careers guidance are not operated on commercial principles in the usual sense of the term but clearly provide services to student and potential and former student, even if these users are not customers in the strictest sense. This is because unlike with catering or student accommodation, there is not an alternative university registry to which students can dissatisfy with the service on offer. Nor are direct payments from users practicable for most of these services. Instead of quality of teaching, students hope a strong emphasis on student social life, the campus environment, accommodation and other non-academic matters.

Also the elements of the student journey service can influence the university student enrollment numbers. First, the application experience covers the interacting between potential students ad institution up to the point of arrival, Second, the academic experience students' interactions with the institution associated with the students, excluding these purposes teaching and learning processes. Finally, the campus experience, student life not connected with study, which may include activities away from the actual campus. Also the graduate students experience, the institution's role is assisting students' transition on employment. For example, all universities can find open days to be valuable recruitment exercises to attract more visitors to applications. The open day can give them a taste of university life and to help in managing their expectations. Potential students frequently used social media sites to obtain more information. As a result, a paid graduate interim, managed by the central marketing department is placed in each academic department with the task of fielding face book and twitter queries from potential and current students . So senior managers need to consider communication with prospective students as a crucial stage in the student journey experiences. Effective communication may reduce the number of students who drop out in their first year. This often happen, it is thought because students come with mistaken expectations that might have been corrected through more effective communications. It is noted, generally that student using these technologies expected instant expense. The management task for the student admissions experience now involves greater emphasis on the presentation of the university, both before and during visits by potential students and their parents more effort given to the induction of students and the management of their expectations and a need to response rapidly to digital queries.

Student university life challenge

Managing student experience in university life

challenge

What factors can influence international student's decision to choose where is abroad study destination . It links to the issue of how universities use knowledge to re-design machine and recruitment strategies towards international students. Commonly, there have three groups of factors that influence international students' decision on study destination which include communication, location and social factors. The sub-categories of these factors include quality of communications, study destination's attractiveness and social network. It is important to any universities need to understand the motivations and reasons international students choose certain programs/courses at a specific university. However, communication factors which has an important influence on international students' decision of study destination. The factors that encourage students to study abroad by examining push and pull factors. The push factors are defined as the factors that operate within the home country and initiate a student's decision to undertake international study when pull factors refer to dimensions within a study destination that make it attractive to international students.

On university communication to international student hand, nowadays, the digital age changes customers' views of convenience, speed, information and service (Armstrong, G, & Kotler, 2007). In fact, student's individual decision also study the existing activities carried out by the university of with regards to marketing and communication for prospective international applicants. The different communication channels to communicate with prospective students by the central unit technology include, such as when participating in education exhibitions and fairs. For example, participation in education exhibitions and fairs internationally in China, India and UK as well as locally is important. Some university department departments join local education exhibitions and fairs. The main purpose is to collect contracts and establish relationships with prospective students. When they return to themselves country, they can then provide further information and answer new queries with follow up email communication. The central unit technology highlights the relevance of parental influence and in certain cultures by targeting parents when who visit education exhibitions and fairs in India and China.

Furthermore, universities need to create a good first impression and build relationship with students, the central unit technology responds promptly to student queries. They understand that a quick and information response is important in separations themselves from their competitors. Prospective students cruise around different websites for information because they want to build relationships with prospective universities and right send email inquiries to several different universities. The university central online unit can join a forum, it is a forum when students/users can post provide assistance to users who have inquiries. For example, university central online unit can start an international ambassador organization. To help with student recruitment during education exhibitions and fairs. Also the university central online unit can maintain a face book page for graduated students. It can serve as an interaction platform for graduated current and prospective students with the university. Such as the central online unit can reach target students from India, China and Europe. They can run a social media challenge on face book that can also reach target UK and Chinese students. So, the university can serve as a pool of information of both current and prospective students. They emphasize that the website is always ranked high among students as a source of information. It is an important channel that provides information which is easily assessment. The following list is the online communication channels used by the different department in university. Such as, email channel is used to answer prospective students' inquiries. Online with universities communication and firms cooperation are introduced to let current students' experiences via recorded video, google advertisements are used to display the university and/or the department as the top option when users search online newsletters and online educational portals are used to connect interested students within specific fields with newsletters via cooperation with online education portals, photo blog. The publish current students' study experiences in the department with photos via blogs. Social media e.g. face book platform is used to provide an interactive platform with students, in special prospective students.

The final one is university website, it is used as the main communication channel link to different departments' own website and provide information. For example, local education exhibitions and fairs can join the central online unit to have face-to-face communication with prospective students, current student network exchange programs and to understand the current international students better, such as via annual brainstorming sessions. Also, lecturers and researcher's online network can promote the university through lecturer exchange and conferences abroad. Industrial network can maintain close relationships with the industries to create chances for students' career prospect.

How can communication channels and marketing communication influence students' decision making on study destination? It focuses on specifying the factors that influence international students' choices to study university destinations. Globalization and internationalization include recruitment of international students, staff exchanges between universities word wide. As globalization, it reflects global competitiveness process. This concept can be applied to consumer behavior theory to education by suggesting that students and their parents go through a few stages and eventually select an institution or subject of study. These stages include, such as pre-search behavior, search behavior, application , choice decision and registration stages. The first stage is pre-search behavior when students are in their early thoughts about their future. Next stage is search behavior stage, in this stage, students will gather information to get the shortlist of the potential study destination, institutions and courses. Then, it is the application stage, who will submit their applications to select institutions in the application stage. Next, it is choice destination occurs when students accept an offer, depending on the number of offers received. Finally, it is the register stage, during the register with the course. It seems the demand for study abroad and competitions in university sector makes international students' preferences an interesting subject to study. Thus, it is important for education marketers to know what factors that influence the purchase with university course choice intention of prospective students .

International student abroad study challenge
In general, students will follow these models to choose course. The first is economic models of student choice, which emphasize the costs aspects in relation to their studies, including the costs of choosing to study instead of work. The second is sociological models of student choice cover issues, such as family influences, personal motivation and ability and other influences. Finally, it is the information processing models of student choice combine both the economic and sociological models to determine the decision making of further study and the selection process of institutions. So, students decide to study abroad which is influences by push and pull factors at different stages. In first stage, students decide to study abroad with the influence of the push factors within the home country. In second stage, involves the selection of the study destination and students evaluate the factors which make one more attractive with pull factors. Lastly, students will select that institutions on third stage and these is additional pull factors make one institutions more attractive than its competitors, such as reputation, school fees, range of courses offered and staff expertise.

Summary, what factors influence students abroad study. There are variety of factors, such as access to local, perception of better quality of overseas teaching system, the availability of technology-based programs, the commonality of language and opportunity to improve second language, the geographic proximity of country, the institution's reputation for quality, the range of available programs/courses and marketing efforts. So, an university's value is based on its relationship building and service delivery towards international students rather than on its facilities and student revenue. The main purpose influences students to further study abroad, especially to achieve personnel satisfaction further career. Commonly, students are buying the benefits that a degree can provide in favor of employment, status and lifestyles. However, influences and recommendations from family members, relatives, friends and professors also play an important role in a student's decision making process to study abroad. For example, Asian and African student are strongly influenced by their family. How universities should influenced by their families? How universities should market themselves to students? For example, Chinese students desire to improve their foreign language skills, are prefer to choose abroad as the study destination. The reasons are that the foreign degrees, e.g. UK are seen to have greater career value than Chinese degrees and that the experiences of living and working. How can attract more international students groups? To achieve this, communication play a crucial role. Communication occurs when a message is sent from a sender to a recipient with a purpose, an expression and a medium in a environment. Internet marketers customize and culture is a collective of interpretations that affects peoples' behaviors. It includes beliefs, values, social practice. They also highlight the link between culture and communication. When communication occurs across the internet, cultural aspects have to be across into account. The reason is the internet offers alternative communication channels like print media, word-of-mouth and public relations. Further, the internet allows markers to customize information that targets different cultures, including both verbal and non verbal content. Then, also highlight the importance of email communication of different languages on the website increases the attraction to receivers. So, it seems internet communication will be an advertisement strategy to assist any university to promote.

According to higher education survey, nearly half of all higher education institutes have experienced enrollment declines and consequently, shortfalls in net tuition revenue goals. Also many colleges need to take roughly 25 to 50% more staff time and effort to give students the levels of client service who expect. There is also no longer a single traditional educational degree. Institutions must accommodate the needs and preferences of students ranging from recent high school graduates to working adult learners. To meet enrollment and budget targets, institutions often attempt to introduce new multiple or double degree programs or to launch broad, institution wide advertising and marketing campaigns. However, it is like reasonable approaches, but results are often varied and unpredictable for two reasons: Such as, when extensive educational market research would give institutions a full understanding of their market opportunities and ideal targets, face have the internet resources necessary to carry it out. Another reason is without data to support their decisions, many institutions implement campaigns that don't differentiate the institution or its programs in ways that reason with today's students.

The key to enrollment growth and competitive strengths in today's higher education market is to offer the right programs to the right students. Using marketing and recruitment strategies in decision making will help boost enrollment, leading to more positive outcomes for both students and institutions. How to identify opportunities for improvements to existing programs that will help attract desired applicants and achieve targeted outcomes ? How to determine a degree program to institution's brand identity? Does a new program suit the institutions brand? Is the program consistent with the institution's loyalty and reputation?

The first suggestion is that researching employer demand for job market. Today, students concern on employment prospects. Corporations that have partnered with an institution can offer valuable insight into their priorities and perspectives on current and upcoming workforce requirements to help the college or university design new programs. Additionally, if particular geographic regions have traditionally provided high volumes of desirable applicants. The institution would gather input from employers to those more markets, then use that information to further refine degree programs to include practical, marketable skills and expertise. For example, incorporating specialties, such as concentrations, certification preparation, or study can help a degree program to develop. Then, collected data might also indicate areas where high schools industries or economic conditions are creating the most likely applicants. So, audience segmentation can include factors, such as political , per capita income, graduate vs undergraduate degrees, media usage and preferences etc.

My another suggestion is concerned these differentiate content for college target audiences, it has two sample categories both, such as first category is career climbers, headline can indicate to how to change course to achieve student individual dreams and to predict where endless opportunities are within reach. So, message can let audiences to feel real life experience and have flexible learning and career connections when who choose to study the university. Second, category is inactive military, headline can indicate to discover new ways to serve and where honor and integrity need precision and performance. So, message can let students to feel to get skills, discipline and experience and the university can have flexible learning options and tuition reimbursement for military service. There are sample communication messaging aligns both with each category and with the institution's existing brand and legacy. How institutions can make smart media choices to students? From owned to earn purchased to traditional, media outlets vary. When a broad mix gives greater exposure, choices should take each person's media preferences and psychological into account. This ensures that each selected channel is appropriate for reaching the target audiences. Also, prospective students can build ongoing relationships with advisors, which increases their engagement as well as institutions can make ongoing improvements by reviewing calls and gaining insight into problems and challenges prospective students may face. The most importance, it is a university can maintain complete records of all contacts. Because accurate, up-to-date records of communication frequency, response rates conversation histories, and schedules follow-up activities can help to ensure timeliness and to the marketing plan.

University life relationship to student challenge

In fact, college planning and management magazine estimates that institutions with " complete customer profiles with accurate data can increase revenue by 66%". So, customer relationship plan can help the university to accomplish to attract university students to enroll to choose to study of this task. Because customer relationship management plan can track such information allowing the recruiting process to run efficiently and making it easier to measure and refine activities that are tied to specific marketing and recruiting tactics. To optimize success, institutions must use research and planning to identify and target student's goals, then follow through with strong, personalized recruitment and enrollment efforts. Some institutions may choose to implement a complete marketing ad recruiting method to most efficiently and effectively make use of valuable resources to a complete marketing and recuritint service plan can help institutions build comprehensive, automized educational market research and recuriting initiative. The result: degree programs optimized for that institution's expertise and reputation and lead generation and recruitment strategies that target the institution's most promising applicants. The practices outlined can make dramatic differences in application volume ans yields when enabling marketing and recruiting efforts to operate more cost effectively and efficiently.

I shall indicate Malaysia educational system for public and private university attractive degree compare to explain why customer (student) relationship management plan is important. Malaysia includes public and private both institutions and it has public and private university, polytechnic, college, non-university status institutions and local or forcing university's branch campus. However, public universities in Malaysiz still attract the majority of undergraduate. Because public universities degree specification are recognized by the public services department, thus, individuals who hold degrees from public universities can work in the public sector, public universities are heavily subsidized by the government are therefore, fees are much cheaper than at private universities. Moreover, public universities can offer more places for professional and critical courses, e.g. medicine, dentistry, pharmaceutical studies, architecture, engineering, law, accounting with qualifications that are mostly and recognized by the respective local professional bodies and public universities provide students with a wider choice of programs in various fields of study.

Student applications for entry into bachelor's degree programs centralized processing agency. The agency of the ministry of higher division of student admission. Applicants need to provide a list of their choice of universities and programs and receive an offer from only one public university. In some case, the offer may even be from a university or program that was not included in the applicant's list of choices. However, the decision students make regarding their education revolves around several issues: first, students who finish their high school education must decide whether to pursue their tertiary education. Second, students who choose to further their education must take a choice regarding their program or field of education and institution of higher education and the institution of higher education.

Thus, in any university's customer relationship management plan, it can consist this first content, such as to find what factors can influence the students' choice of this specific institution of higher education. The tertiary institution choice modes include the following: economic models, sociological and combined models. Economic models of human capital investment emphasize rational decision ranking behavior when examining student's college choice. Students choose a college based on the level of value that each institution offers by comparing costs with perceived benefits. If the students feel the benefits of attending the institution are greater than the perceived benefits of enrolling in order institution. The contribution of human capital investment factors, e.g. family income, tuition and financial aid on enrolments. For example, Ellwood and kane (2000) used a human capital income and college enrollment when controlling for academic ability, tuition and financial aid and preference (measured by parental education). Although the human capital investment model shows the effects of variables like income and ability on college related decision, it has limited usefulness in explaining source of difference in college choices across groups.

Next, in any university's customer relationship management plan, it can consist this second content, such as to find how to make the students choose this college to study. The combined models show a diversity of factors that influence students' choices. Some factors are related to the role of other persons, some are related to personal or individual factors and others are related to institutional characteristics and student perceptions about value and costs. Usually university causes negative relationship is caused by reputation of the institution, the program structure, the quality of the lecturers or families, the influence of the student's family and friends and customers (students) orientation in terms of entry (enrolling) requirement and availability of courses, courses fees, online or classroom teaching method, campus location etc. factors.

In general, the Asia country, Malaysia students concern these issues before who choose to study the university. The factors include: the demographic profile of the students, e.g. gender, age, ethnicity, the socio-economic background of the family, e.g. household income and parent education level and occupation, the reasons of the student pursue a higher education, the sources of information used in choosing a university college, and the factors that influence students' choice between public and private tertiary institutions etc. factors. All those factors will influence the Malaysia student who decides to choose to study the public or private tertiary institution finally. So, in their choosing procedure, Malaysia students will consider that factors are the importance of the various reasons for furthering whose education and then to specify which of the reasons is the most important.

Commonly Malaysia students who will consider whether the university will help them to find a good job, increase knowledge and to gain experience. Other reasons include fulfilment of parental expectations, interest in the field of study, enjoyment of campus life and the influence of their friends. In fact, Malaysis students can choose either of a public or private university to study. The factors influence them to choose include: the quality of education, lower tuition fee and access to financial assistance. However, the financial factors, e.g. lower tuition fee of education and available financial assistance in public institutions are extremely important considerations to influence their choice. Other factor is the quality of education provided by the public or private university. The key performance indicators (kpds) report indicated that students in public universities are assured of receiving high quality tertiary education because the efficiency and productivity of public universities, that encompass various aspects, such as teaching and learning, employability of students and social responsibility (Universiti, Teknologi MARA, 2009).

In general, for science students, who will concern about whether the university can provide enough facilities to have been made available to them to carry on researching in campus environment, which include the following: teaching facilities, computer and research laboratories, lecture hall, complex equipped with state of the art multimedia systems etc. excellent library facilities, sports facilities and other supporting facilities, such as a book store, a health center and book services.

Finally, I suggest university information ought to be highlighted in university's website because the internet and university websites are the source of information must frequently used by students to make their choice of tertiary education institution. Because students consider the availability of a course or program that who wish to pursue as another extremely important consideration to study in Malaysia public or private university. However, it is necessary to keep abreast with changes in the higher education and the contemporary demands from the working world require review of program and courses. To design new courses that balance the diverse needs of students and the emerging needs of the educational and labor markets in Malaysia. For example, the school of social sciences in Malaysia university, which is the focus of this study is planning in the near future to introduce two new program. Bachelor of social work program and a bachelor of Economics program. The two new courses will include various courses in new areas of study that are emerging in these disciplines.

To conclude, new to focus on various factors in order to attract students of high quality to its undergraduate courses, the university will be able to nurture students for post graduate studies higher education program as a research university. Such as in Malaysia rapidly growing education sector, it must transform itself into a world class university, so that it can attract the best students and produce the best graduates in the country.

Finally, in the university's client relationship management plan, it needs to find what the variety of trends to develop recruitment and technology and enrollment and branding within higher education marketing is for the university. Nowadays, the variety of trends to higher education marketing. Such as many universities have hires marketing professionals from the corporate world, who have invested significant time and money to create strong institutional brands. The online and digital space is using technology to its full potential, particularly with social media and other platforms, for graduates recruitment service in universities. Also, recruitment strategies in higher education increasingly focus on international students and non-traditional and adult learners.

Online of continuing education program will be popular to be taught to online students. Adaptive learning technology has also enjoyed significant interest to let students feel new learning method. Successful branding and marketing have become increasingly important activities for institutions. Every university needs to differentiate itself from computer institutions. Successful branding can help with increasing enrollment, expanding fundraising capabilities, and other outcomes.

How to communicate a brand to build confidence and famous university image to students? However, there is evidence that universities don't have to spend significant amounts of money to promote online advertisement to be effective. For example, institutions need image have more emphasis on responsive web design to create university online advertisement and easy to navigate websites that can viewed on multiple devices and platforms. Also administrators want their universities to receive a prominent spot in search engine results particularly googles. Especially for institutions that offer niche courses. It is increasingly important to ensure that research results include these courses at the top rank. Also, colleges and universities can rely on data driven analytics to determine who, how and where who are reaching their audiences. The use of analytics software is increasing as the higher education web ecosystem is becoming expanding (domains, subdomains etc.) Getting a better handle of this data is a new area of concentration for colleges and universities.

Some form of social media, e.g. face book or twitter accounts will be popular to accept to attract to see university's online advertisement. Also the rise of mobile technology and connected devices, colleagues and universities are making greater investments in having a mobile presence. This includes not only mobile versions of university websites and other content. Beyond, the changes are brought by teaching, marketing and branding trends have shown more creatively outreach efforts, as well as design and advertising campaigns. However, more traditional marketing and branding strategies, such as open house events and sponsored visits for students are also extremely popular.

I feel any university needs to build its brand to let different country's students know. Branding requires patient and effort and relies heavily on timing. A university brand can be damaged much more quickly than it can be successfully built. So, consistency purpose and messaging is necessary. For instance, a series of low university rankings can do long term damage to the image. It is very important to keep promises, particularly when it comes to the quality of the education provided. Institutions must be committed to maintaining and improving quality. Universities' communications must constantly be facts, data and evidence: rankings, applicant data (number and quality), recruitment of professors, placement of graduates, media presence, that demonstrates the quality, as the excellence of the institutions helps and strengthens its brand for long term.

One of the most significant ways branding and marketing of higher education has changed in recent years has been in the online space, using a variety of new platforms for external social and digital platforms. To achieve this, it ahs become common for universities to ensure home page is clearly laid out portal to all of the content that students are looking for online. This means websites often have new feature elements, such as well placed navigation bars and engaging visuals, e.g. slideshow, multimedia, content etc. So, broader tends in the use of social media platforms, however, have shown that when their use of colleges, universities, community colleges and other academic institutions. Also, there are a number of tends in recruitment and enrollment that are having a significant impact on how institutions go about attracting. There are a number of trends in recruitment and enrollment students knowing consumers' education tuition what level is reasonable issue is important factor, that are having a significant impact on how institutions go about attracting students. It includes demographics and increased mobility of students, as well as the increasing cost of higher education in many countries.

Firstly, I shall indicate the recent higher education trends for enrollment and recruitment references hand. Such as: education cost trend, effect or impact to many families concern experiencing a diminished ability to pay for a college education compared to pre-recession levels, median household income, home equity and net worth are all down. Meanwhile, commonly global college tuition costs have continued to climb steadily, even after financial aid is factored in. Even more families are re-evaluating the education tuition, who are willing to pay for a college education. Commonly, the cost of a college education is climb up against the ceiling of what education. The cost of a college education is climbing up against the ceiling of what families will consider paying. Even, students from upper-middle income families are experiencing higher levels of student debt and factoring in the cost of post-graduate study of majoring in certain fields. So what major subject choice at the course factor will influence the student feel whether the tuition is reasonable or unreasonable to pay. Even, media coverage and legislative attention are shaping public opinion about the value of a college education is necessary a value gap which has opened up in the polling because far fewer people believe going to college at any price will be worth the financial investment. It seems some public universities which get government funders' assistance can make their appropriations contingent upon institutional better performance measures. In fact, families are seeking evidence of successful results to justify their college investment. Higher education has become less and end itself and increasingly a means to an end primarily an economically viable career factor in outcomes as well as cost. Students will expect proof of high graduation rates and graduate employment at acceptable salary levels.

Secondly, on different demographics trend hand, the number of high school graduates is shrinking, but the proportion that is ethically diverse is growing. The country's changing demographics, combined with a widening gap between the nation's rich and poor, mean more first generation students and students from socio-economic background that not only make paying for college a challenge, but also often leave them underprepared for college level study.

Thirdly, In the study aging trend hand, non-traditional age students still represent a largely expanding market. During the economic recession, more people age 25 and older returned to college, but that reached its peak in 2020 year prior record. But nontraditional students also more likely to leave out in their first year. So who seek convenient course scheduling, assistance is the financial aid process, tutoring ad counseling services.

Fourthly, on the transfers of university hand, more students are attending multiple institutions in their pursuit of a degree. Transferring is increasingly becoming a cost-conscious part of students' long term plans to affordable degree completion. In general, students who transfer from a private non profit institution attend two year public institutions, with four year public institutions being their second most popular destination. On university student of consumption behavior engaged consumers hand, growth in mobile online access and social media use is allowing people to instantly verify any claims a college makes.

Generation connected is not bound by age brackets, but rather by shared behavior, this is used of real time social, local and mobile technology. They find it increasingly easy to investigate institution's reputations via online networks, word-of-mouth recommendations and other communication channels beyond the colleges' direct control. Students like to investigate any universities' target data from internet channels.

The widespread use of data analytics in other industries is leading students to expect personalized and relevant communications. The digital information that can be captured about even those students who don't explicitly make their interest known to be college has enhanced targeting capabilities. And since private non profit institutions are known for providing personal attention, families do note any disconnects in that any university brand attribute during the admissions process.

Finally, on the online education trend, the proliferation of massive open online courses is drawing attention to how college credits are awarded. All types of online and hybrid courses are be popular to university marketplace seeks cost effective access and convenient delivery. So the university student segment will be popular to online courses teaching channel to any international college in the future. Also, advertising is important promotion method to let students know that the university is update message. Among the least effective strategies and tactics for both private and public four year institutions were radio advertising, the popular advertising will be online college fairs and billboard/ bus/outdoor advertising. However, running television advertisement was rested a top practice, it is possible that television advertising can give visual enjoyment to attract student audience attention. Also the preferred method of communication with potential students, it will be sending email , however, though mailers and brochures are still used by a significant number of institutions.

The international university education competition, among the most competitive areas of colleges and universities increasingly across the globe is the international/foreign student market. The U.S., Britain, Australia and other English speaking countries are competing for largely the same students and some warn that the number of courses available to international students in these countries will outstrip the number of students on the education market. So, the combination of increased mobility of students and the lower number of first time applicants at universities in English speaking countries has created pressures to compete for international students. In addition, any country also needs have good marketing and recruitment strategy for graduate students. It aims to attract international students. For example, some institutions have elected to hire companies, such as the Pearson employment firm's progression and "website gives students most likely exam clients admission and " pathway information on universities that partner with Pearson.

The U.S. has been particularly success in its recruitment of international students, particularly Chinese students. To achieve Chinese student to choose U.S. institutions have had to change their strategies for recruitment, such as maintaining a presence at conferences and job fairs overseas offering generous financial aid packages to international students as well as improving social media outreach effort. Some university students who are adult learners. Outside of international student recruitment trends in higher education indicate that another key audience for enrollment is adult and non traditional learners.

In the United States, the number of adult learners returning to higher education. So, the student individual age will be increased to 25 age and over and this pattern is expected to continues. The reason is possible that some adult students who are working and who feel whose employers need them to raise knowledge to achieve the educational acceptance level to feel who has effort to do the job. It will predict that the percentage of enrollments for students 25 age and older will increase by 20% over 2010 year. So, it will be global education trend, the adult student target segment will increase in global education market. However, recruiting those adult students will encounter an unmet demand and growing market segment for both countries and who required recruitment strategies that speak directly to this demographic. When some of the employment methods are the same as recruiting traditional students , e.g. quality, communication methods, effective websites, using social media etc. other trends are noticeable in how institutions make their programs more attractive to adult learners. zone of the most common course design to highly flexible programs that can meet the needs of working adult learners, including expanding offering in the part and evening course different adult student segment needs and to satisfy the number of options for online education. Additional improving lead educational quality when identifying adult students and designing adult learn programs specifically adult students as opposed to adopt existing programs.

In summary, University (education) industry examines the effects of lowered admissions standards on universities facing both lower graduation rates and reductions in state funding. For university rank, international student, in special Asian or non english nature language students, who choose overseas universities to enroll, who will concern the institutions. So universities can provide to relax standards in other areas to boost their international enrollments in particular, such as required language proficiency, in favor of admitting those students that exhibit strong academic backgrounds. A trend in recent years for U.S. institutions has been to admit international students with weak language skills about strong academic skills on a conditional basis, allowing students to strengthen language abilities once admitted. These types of admissions are often called " intensive English enrollments" and several institutions have reported a distinct increase in enrollments as a result of such admissions policies that feature language programs. Hence, if the university required high level English language proficiency ability to enroll to study any courses, then it will attract more potential English language students to enroll in this global competition education market. Otherwise, the lower English language level institutions will encounter to loss more. Besides, the classroom which typical lecture and homework of a a course are reversed and in classroom experiences reconstructed to rely less on passive learning and more an active engagement. Because university students concern how to consume the core elements of a course whenever, regardless of time or place. This mean professors can re-allot classroom time completely and make a room for other activities, such as experimental or collaborative learning opportunities as opposed to passive learning through lecturers.

Thus, it seems how university can attract more students to study, it depends on lecturer's individual teaching method or choosing what kind of education courses to be taught to whose students. It will influence students have good or bad emotion or feeling to learn. So, university needs to concern lecturer's teaching methods to let students to feel satisfactory. Also, where the university campus location choice is another factor to influence student choice as well as student learning experience to the university etc. factors will be the most influential to any students to choose which university to study finally. So, educators need to concern these issues.

Education and economy challenge influences
developing country student psychology

Researching the relationship between education and economy how to influence developing country student psychology nowadays. This topic is concerned how to use labor economy method to analyze how to influence Asia country student psychology challenge. I shall indicate some developing countries in Asia, e.g. Philippines, Korea, China etc. countries. What the link between education and productivity and student psychology is? What does the model that characterize key featured of growth processes of Asia countries are? For this topic, I shall suppose human capital is come from such as primary and secondary and tertiary education factor which has a major close relationship to cause each student psychology nowadays. My objectives of this research are to explore the relationship between graduates psychology and educational productivity and quality , assess what should be the key variable (or variables) of interest and quantify and qualify the relationship to influence student studying psychology.

Education challenge influences development country student psychology

Human capital has ability and efficiency of labor to transform raw materials and capital into products and services to affect economic growth. The accumulation of human capital improves labor productivity and increases the returns to capital. However, a well educated background is essential to raise technology to develop economic growth in Asia developing countries especially.

In macro and micro economic view, the well educated labor (human capital) is often as one of the critical factors to influence rapid economic growth to the Asia developing countries' any regions or cities. Because any of these Asia developing countries, such as China, Korea, Philippines etc. countries which need have well educated and knowledgeable labors to raise any employers' productivities and income growth. So productivity and education qualify factor which ought have close relationship to cause student studying psychology in any one of Asia developing countries.

For example, China was an major industrial and farming country between 1960 year and 2000 year. However, after 2000 year, it began to achieve any commercial investment to raise GDP income and to raise more service provision nature of employment chance to domestic labors. e.g. financial investment, shares trading, hotels and tourism and airlines and restaurants and cinemas etc. service nature businesses commercial investment. Moreover, the foreign investors were also attracted to set up factories to manufacture their products in China's country any area locations. It was possible that this foreign investors felt China's workers' wages were more cheaper than themselves domestic worker wages. For example, USA has the minimum wage legislation to protect it's domestic individual worker wage level. Otherwise, China's individual worker wage level is compared to be paid more lower level to compare to USA's minimize legislative individual worker wage level nowadays. It seems China, Korea, Philippines etc. Asia developing countries need have well educated labors to help them to develop economic growth because good education quality can influence student studying psychology.

Because the developed countries' foreign well educated labors, e.g. USA, UK etc. who feel whose countries can give the best salary compensation level and benefits to let them to support to work and to live in whose countries. So the developed countries' well educated labors won't choose to go to China to work very easily. It seems those developing Asia countries which governments need to invest in education sector to increase many knowledgeable human labors capital to assist them to raise whose technological productivity or service productivity or factory productivity to raise student learning emotion and effort to achieve economic growth for long term. If any one of these Asia developing Asia countries still want to keep the competitive position in global environment in the future , these Asia developing countries must need good education labors to provide good quality of education to train any aspects of high knowledgeable labors to supply to themselves society to work in essential.

Education quality and student learning emotion challenge

Ha, Kim and Lee (2009) provided evidence to indicate that "using panel data covering from 1989 year to 2000 year in Japan, Korea and Taipei, China as the distance to the technology frontier narrows basis research and development (R&D) investment, i.e. highly skilled labor which showed the higher growth effect than development R&D investment , i.e. less skilled labor. They also provided evidence that the quality of tertiary education has a significantly positive effect on the productivity of R&D.

Nowadays, education is commonly regarded as the most direct influence to people out of poverty owing to the tendency for employment opportunities especially for higher skilled workers to be created in Asia developing countries. In fact, raising productivity is depended on the quantity and quality of human resource, which itself largely depends on investment in education theoretical linkages between education and growth. Generally, growth theory suggests that economic growth depends on the accumulation of economic, including human assets and the return on these assets, which depend on technological progress, the efficiency which assets are being used. So, growth theory which emphasizes on the centrality of human capital for innovation and technological progress. However, the theory indicates of policy ineffectiveness which characterizes the neo-classical growrh theory by giving importance to the production of new technologies and human capital development. So focusing on factors within the model rather than relying on external factors. It seems the economists of supporting growth believe that improvements in productivity are linked to a faster pace of innovation and extra investment in human capital. Also these economists of supporting growth theory emphasize on the need for governments and private sector educational institutions and job markets for tertiary students' demand and to innovate knowledgeable of social economy to actively provide incentives for individual student to become inventive in any countries. They also identify the central role of knowledge as determinant of economic growth. Hence, growth theory can predict positive externalities and spillover effects from development of a high valued-added knowledge economy to the development and maintenance of a competitive advantage across the global.

Why do I research the relationship between education and productivity can influence the economic growth to Asia developing countries? Although, human capital includes education, health and aspects of social capital. The main focus of the present study is on education. The analysis stresses the destination between the quantity of education measured by years of attainment at various levels and the quality measured by scores on internationally comparable examinations, e.g. China education and Korea education compare. In fact, the global long term economic growth was the central macroeconomic problem and it was fortunately accompanied in the late 1980 year by importance advances in the theory of economic growth. This period featured the development of global growth models, in which the long term rate of growth was determined within the model.

A key feature of these models is a theory of technological progress, viewed as a process whereby purposeful research and application lead over time to new and better products and methods of production by developed economic globalization. The recent growth models are useful for understanding why advanced economies and the world is as whole, can continue to grow in the long run despite the workings of diminishing returns in the accumulation of physical and human capital. These countries include, e.g. America, England which are observed to be rich and high tend also to be those that have high long run target levels of per high capita output in a setting that includes human capital and technological change. So education is also essential to raise labor knowledge and technological level to assist developed countries, e.g. USA, UK , to raise productivity to achieve economic growth. So, the developed or developing countries' both government policies and education institutions need to concern their national population to arrange the different primary, secondary and tertiary educational policy to educate to develop whose students to develop different professional and knowledgeable and skillful abilities to already develop their careers in different nature of jobs to enter their societies to work nowadays. However, if we were the identify how education contributes to cause economic growth in any Asia developing countries. We need to compare states that have a similar distance to the frontier and yet choose difference pattern of investment in education. For example, building a new school for a research university, the process is when a vacancy arises on an committee that controls expenditure. Because governments and universities need to concern what the labour market demand, so the research university can decide prefer to choose what kinds of subjects to be taught to its potential students, e.g. medical or architect or law or engineering or business or social science, computer science etc. subjects among of them subjects, which subjects will be chosen to be taught to its potential students preferably. So, the job demand market research is very important because it can help the research university to choose what the preferable subjects will be demanded to supply to the labor market increasing in any one of Asia developing countries within future three or five years.

Theories of economic growth have emphasized the role of human capital which may affect economic growth. Human capital is as an extra input in the aggregate production function, where the output of the means economy is a direct function of factor inputs: physical capital, labor and human capital. However, technologies can raise innovate capacity of economy through developing new ideas. So, education was seemed that it could be raised graduated students' abilities to raise productivity to any one of Asia developing countries by high technological skill.

Long run economic growth challenge influences to education provision to developing Asia countries

Any countries have two different channels through which human capital can affect long run economic growth by education provision. The first channel is when human capital is a direct input in the production function and the second channel is when the human capital affects the technology parameter. The result establishes a long run relationship between education and economic growth. A well-educated labor force appears to significantly influence economic growth both as a factor in the production function and through total factor productivity. With its large resources of human and natural resources, the potential to build a prosperous economy to reduce poverty significantly and to provide the health, education services that its population needs. As the Asia developing countries, e.g. China or Korea, which are poor countries past years, which need foreign investors' different businesses development in their countries. So, themselves education is commonly regarded as the most direct avenue to rescue a substantial number of people out of poverty since there is likely to be more employment opportunities and higher wages for skilled workers. Furthermore, education can enable children's attitudes and assists them to grow up with social values that are more beneficial to their nations and themselves.

The theoretical basis of education on economic growth is rooted in the endogenous growth theory. Endogenous growth economists believe that improvements in productivity can be linked to a faster pace of innovation and extra investment in human capital. Growth theorists argue the need for government and private sector institutions and markets which need to innovate and provide incentives for individuals to be inventive. There is also a central role for knowledge as a determinant of economic growth theory can predict positive externalities and spill over effects from development of a high valued-added knowledge economy which is able to develop and maintain a competitive advantage in growth industries in the global economy.

Nowadays, education at levels countries to economic growth through imparting general attitudes and discipline and special skills necessary for a variety of work places. It contributes to economic growth by improving health, reducing fertility and possibly by contributing to political stability to different developing or developed both countries. The major importance of the educational system to any labor market would depend majority in ability to produce a literate, disciplines, flexible labor force via high quality education. Consequently, with economic development new technology is applied to production with results in an increase in the demand for workers and better education. In the developing countries, e.g. China, Korea, rich individuals allocate labor time not only for their own production and knowledge accumulation, but also train the poor individuals. In the past, some economists estimated a model of economic growth and human capital accumulation based on a sample of developing countries, e.g. China, Korea etc. are not a different stage of development. Their result revealed that the increase in the primary and secondary countries to an increase in productivity. They indicate that human capital accumulation rates are affected by demographic variables. For example, they established that an increase in life expectancy at birth brings about an increase in secondary and tertiary education when a decrease in the dependence rate negatively affects secondary education. Finally, they added that geographic variables have a considerable importance in the human capital accumulation process. Nevertheless, studies differed on the impact of human capital on productivity.

The economists also indicate that human capital accumulation rates are affected by demographic variables as well as the increase in the primary and secondary level of education contributes to an increase in productivity. For example, they established that a increase in life expectancy at birth brings about an increase in secondary and tertiary education when a decrease in the dependence rate negatively affects secondary education. However, who also believe the overall results of secondary and higher education can have a significant positive impact on growth, when primary education had not contributed to economic growth.

Productivity and economic growth challenge measures to developing countries educational system
The GDP per unit of labor input should be related to the share of labor of a particular type (graduates or workers at different qualification levels) weighted by the average human capital of the type of worker (captured by the relative wages of different types of labor input). It seems measure of the relationship between education and productivity and economic growth can be quantified clearing to developing Asia any countries.
In past, the EUKLEMS project indicated key findings of 15 developed countries for one economic report: GDP per employment hour increased from 1992 year to 2005 year, the highest annual average percentage change was in Finland (2.7%), Japan (2.5%) and the UK (2.4%). These countries had the lowest level of GDP per employment hour in 1982 year, when the period considered the Netherlands and the USA had the highest GDP employment hour. Also it indicated the share of employment with tertiary education also increased from 1982 year to 2005 year in all countries. The highest annual average percentage change was in Australia (5%) followed by the UK (4.9%). Both of these countries had relatively low shares of employment with tertiary education in 1982 year at 6%, compared with 22.1% in the USA and 18.7% in Finland. The large increased closed the gap, but the USA and Finland still had higher employment shares with tertiary education than Australia and the UK in 2005 year. The economic report also indicatd that a 1% increase in the share of the workforce with a university degree raises the level of long run productivity by 0.2%-0.5%. So, it implied the education and productivity has close relationship to developed countries also. However, the economic benefits, both to the individual and to the wider economy of a university degree with clearly depend on the quality and skills to developing and developed countries both.
So, improvement in educational outcomes have been widely recognized as essential in enhancing growth in both developed and developing countries. In fact, education is acquire by individuals provide social returns at the macroeconomic level and addition indirect benefits to economic growth.

Measurement growth rate of productivity to Asia educational system
Firstly, I suppose it has relationship between human capital and education has close relationship to cause economic growth to any developed or developing countries both nowadays. Because if human capital and

education factor has close relationship to influence any country's economic growth, then it is possible to cause productivity and economic growth has close relationship. However, some economists indicate the evidence on the relationship between human capital and economic growth and who conclude that there is strong evidence that human capital increases productivity. Suggesting that education really is productivity-enhancing, rather than education is used by individuals to signal their ability to potential employers.

The primary measures are used to capture the average level of human capital per worker include:

● The average number of years of schooling of the workforce or population, which assumes a linear relationship with human capital.

● The share of the workforce population with specific educational qualifications.

● School enrolment rates, specially as a starting value. This flow into education is often used as stock of qualifications and is available for developed Asia countries, e.g. Hong Kong, Japan and developing Asia countries, e.g. China, Korea both.

However, developing Asia countries have potential problems arising from measurement errors in education, as the average schooling levels are derived from enrolment flows. They adopt more reliable country level education micro data and find a positive result or response between the growth rate of education and economic growth. Human capital flows are most commonly provided by school enrolment rates, have been widely used in studies of the relationship between human captial and growth. This is largely due to the availability of long time series of data for a large developing or developed both Asia or foreign countries rather than because it is viewed as proferable to the human captial stock of education measures. So, based on the motivation that school enrolment rates conflate human capital stock and accumulation effects and lead to misinterpretations of the role of labor force growth. It seems education may be one of method to raise human capital and productivity growth to cause any developed or developing Asia or foreign countries' economic growth for long term nowadays.

Economic challenge influences to developing countries' educational system

Recently, the research indicates the impact of education quality is mixed. Moreover, recent studies actually suggest that education quantity is unrelated to economic growth at least in developed countries. On the other hand, a growing literature focuses on the growth impact of education quality, measures by international test scores. It finds a strong effect of education quality on economic growth when confirming that education quantity is irrelevant apart from via its impact on quality. So, I suggest the developing Asia countries' governments, e.g. China, Korea should continue their market based reforms in education. For example, by streamlining the requirements and process to establish new free schools. The goals should be to expand parental choice as widely as possible. Because education might be way to personal fulfilment, but it can also be an instrument for a healthy economy. So, reforming the education system could be a key part of any long term growth strategy to any Asia developing countries. For example, whose governments can increase spending significantly, when gradually raising the compulsory education age from 16 to 18 age following the education and skills act. Also expanding the average number of years spent in education be sufficient to improve growth. Also, any one of Asia developing countries can raise education quality more important that how much education one receives , i.e. education quantity? And how education policy can secure the highest economic dividend in as reduce efficient manner as possible. The policy implication is clear the Asia developing countries' governments should encourage an increase in the enrolment shares of independently operated schools, for example by streamlining the requirements and process to establish new free schools. A voucher system with which pupils can attend the school of their choice, either public or independent would be preferable. Such a system would sharpen competitive incentives in the education system significantly. Thus increasing the potential for choice to produce an economic dividend.

Why is education presumed to affect economic growth in any one of Asia developing countries? The main reason given is that it should improve the overall skill level, or human capital of the labor force. How human capital may be related to economic growth. Usually, capital growth is only determined by capital accumulation and technological changes. In the growth model, only technological innovation can explain long term growth because capital accumulation effects suffer from diminishing and returns. Technological change is thus the sole determinant of growth once an economy's new equilibrium/steady state (zero growth states is reached. At the same time, the sources of technological change, such as human capital are assumed to be not included as an explanatory variable in the model. In other words, the model treats education as a residual rather than as integral part of the process of change in explaining an economy's per-capita growth rate. Thus, some economists do not believe education is a conceptual tool to assist economic growth. However, some economists believe technological change and education can assist economic growth when these two factors are same to exist. Thus, education can impact growth not only by affecting innovation directly. But also by aiding the adoption of existing technology. The augmented assumed that the effect of education eventually growth models allow education at any given level to continue to impact growth through its effect on technological change and diffusion in the economy. In other meaning, education can be provide to students to raise high technological human capital to assist economic growth. So, education can be treated as a regular factor of production to affect the growth rate in the subsequent period. This has implications for how the education variable should be included in statistical analyses, which has been a subject of debate. Otherwise, most research has focused mostly on education quantity,such as the average number of years of schooling. For example, some older studies used school enrolment rates as a measure of education. Enrolment rates impacts are being used different growth periods average over the period. It also indicates that increasing enrolment rates are positive for economic growth in developing Asia countries, e.g. China , Korea etc. In conclusion, it seems education quantity and quality as well as productivity has also relationship to influence developing Asia countries' economic growth for long term.

Raise Teaching Quality challenge

Interactive lecturing strategy challenge

I shall recommend interactive lecturing strategies to raise teaching quality. How to apply interactive lecturing strategies to raise participation in large group presentation? The use of interactive lecturers can promote active learning, high attention and motivation, give feedback to the teacher and the student, and increase techniques that can be used in large group presentations to achieve learning satisfaction for both.

For medical subject education example, interactive lecturing involves a two way interaction between the presenter and the participants (medical students). Interaction can also refer medical teaching material or the medical teaching content of a medical lecture. It does not necessary mean the talking. In all cases, however, interactive lecturing is implied active involvement and participation by the medical student (audience), so the medical students are no longer passive in the learning process. In giving this type of medical presentation, the medical " instructor" frequently becomes a " facilitator" or coach and more often than not, has to modify (change) the medical lecture content to allow for discussion and try new medical technique. Because medical students need to carry on medical practicing, so for any purpose of medical discussion and try new medical technique, refer to any large group medical presentation. It is important to note, however, that the number of medical students in the audience does not dictate whether the medical lecture can be interactive. Some way small medical student groups can be non-interactive, and certain interactive medical techniques can be incorporated into a class of over 200 medical students. Moreover, although large medical classes are most commonly considered the medical content for interactive lecturers, these medical techniques can also be used effective with smaller medical groups in the universities.

Why does university need an interactive lecture and how can it raise teaching quality? One of the major reasons for this critique is observation that lecturers are less effective than other methods when instructional goals involve the application of information or facts. However, when many teachers accept the notion that other teaching methods might be better than lecturers for encouraging students to be more actively involves in learning and for promoting the application of knowledge few have the time, resources or opportunity to use the small group methods to teach. Also, when done effectively, lecture can transmit new information in an efficient way, who can explain or clarify difficult notions, organize concepts and thinking, challenge beliefs, model problem solving and motive students to learn more easier from interacting lecturing. The value of interactive lecturing can let students have active participation and learning beyond the recall of facts and that students must be attentive and motivated in order for learning to occur. However, interactive lecturing can promote active involvement with the teaching can promote active material or the content, with the teacher or with classmate/peers.

Is teaching in class often simulated by questions or problem solving exercises as the students think about what who would answer in a particular situations? I feel these talking performance will increase attention and motivation to students and interactive lecturing strategy can encourage students to participate to ask questions in classroom. Because motivation is the essential ingredients for learning and often is more than intelligence to the student. I feel interactive lectures can simulate interest and help to maintain attention. By encouraging student to talk in classroom to be apply to feel life situations or focusing to use interactive lecturers in methods to motivate students read and learn more. How to evaluate interactive lecturing to facilities? In fact, interactive lecturing can facilitate these teaching material presented. It also assist teachers and students to solve problem and to assist to make decision, communication skills in classroom more easy. This is particularly important in medical education where the application of use of information is as important as recall of patient records of facts to carrying on researching. Moreover, interactive techniques allow teachers to receive feedback at a number of levels: on students needs (at the beginning, middle or end of a lecture), students on the other hand, can get feedback on their own knowledge or performance. In summary, participation on the part of the teacher interactive lecturing encourages active participation on the part of the teacher and the student. This method of teaching encourages student attention and allows for instant feedback on whether the lecture material has been understood.

How are commonly used from interactive techniques? These interactive teaching techniques have multiple benefits, so the instructor can easily and quickly assess of students have really mastered the studying materials and plan to dedicate move time to it, if necessary and the process of measuring student understanding in many cases is also practice for the study materials, often students don't actually learn the study material until of these assessments drives interactivity and brings several benefits. These interactive teaching techniques can let students feel more fun to listen a lecture to teach attentively in classroom.

The lecture instructor action includes, such as at the first, showing picture is as an image to students with no explanation, and asking them to identify or explain it and to justify their answers. Or asking students to write it using terms from lecture, or to name the processes and concepts down. Also, works are well as group activity. The lecturer can not give the answer to let students to know until who have explored all options first. At the second point, lecturer can ask a rhetorical question, and then allow 15-25 seconds, for students to think about the problem before the lecturers hope to wait to explain the question.

The technique encourages students to participate in the problem solving process, even when discussion isn't feasible to let students to write any questions and the lecturer also writes an answer or the same time. It aims to help assure that the students will work in fact on the problem. At the third point, the lecturer can ask a one word answer will suggest degree of comprehension. It aims to help students can learn to remember any new word easily. At the forth point, the instructors can illustrate a concept, idea or principle with a real life application model or cause study. The lecturer distribute a partially completed outline of today's lecture and ask student to fill it in. Useful at start or at end of class, which any student can write down personal opinion which concerns any controversial subject, then during finishing to teach any whole course in the end of the seminar. So the lecturer can gather all classroom opinion polls to aim to let the school to know what the students' feeling concern on the lecturer's teaching performance and the controversial subject content whether who feel more or less interest to learn their subject. Then, the school can evaluate whether it needs to change the subject's teaching contents or the lecturer's teaching method to satisfy whose further learning needs. At the fifth point, let students have chanced to perform whose feeling, e.g. students can either stand or sit to indicate whose answers, such as true or false to the instructor's questions, the lecturer can select some students to travel the classroom polling the others on a topic relevant to the course, then report back the results for everyone. At the sixth point, the lecturer can prepare a questionnaire for students that probes what kind of learning style who use, so the course can match visual learning styles. Also, the lecturer can provide a quote relevant to whose topic, but leave out a crucial word and ask students to guess what it might be. It aims to raise students interesting to learn the topic of contents. Then, the lecturer can ask the class to examine two written out version of a theory or law of nature concept etc. Where one is incorrect, such as the opposite or negation of the other. In deciding which is correct, students will have to examine the problem from all investigations. The lecturer design class activities or even essays to address the real lives of the individual students. Finally, the lecturer ought let student to perform these five steps: listen, stop, reflect, write, give feedback. So students can become self monitoring listeners Focused list several ideas related to the main focus point, helpful for starting new topics and using questionnaire (multi-choice or short answer). When introducing a new topic, assesses interest and preparation for the course, keeping track of the steps needed to solve specific types of problems. Model a list for students first and then asking them to perform similar steps.

Why do lecturers need to be trained to raise teaching quality? Nowadays, it is common that many small in scale, low in credibility and poorly supported educational institutions, are carrying on substantial training of 120 to 500 hours duration, is often compulsory and is sometimes linked to probation to lecturers. Increased confidence in the value of such training has not, however been based on solid evidence regarding the impact of training on teaching learning. Studies tend not to obtain evidence from theoretically or based questionnaires, obtain evidence from students or obtain evidence about impact on student learning to decide whether lecturers need to be trained. Education trainers are often articulate about what who are trying to achieve from their training methods and are finding whether who are trained successful. Education training is capable of achieving three of these goals: the improvement of teachers' skills; the development of teachers' conceptions of teaching and learning; consequent changes in students' learning. Other common goals of training, such as developing teachers' ability to reflect and be self-improving or to increasing self- confidence or self-efficiency , were not studied.

A teacher's approach to teaching has been shown to relate to the approach to study of their students, student-focused teachers are more likely to have students who take a deep approach (attempting to make sense of content) rather than a surface approach (attempting to remember content) (Trigwell et., 1999). However, much training is oriented towards developing teachers' teaching skills, especially whose classroom practice. Measures of teaching behavior have been shown to correlate with various measures of learning outcome. Some trainers need various measures of learning outcome. Some trainers are primarily oriented towards improving student learning, rather than towards improving teaching, and so their training is oriented towards changing teachers so that who are oriented towards student learning rather than towards teaching as performance.

Attractive course content and learning
method raises teaching quality challenge

One of the most notable trends in higher education branding and marketing is that institutions and dedicating more attention to hire marketing professionals from the corporate and have invested significant time and money to create strong institutional brands to build excellent teaching quality image. Perhaps the largest area of innovation and growth in higher education marketing and branding as well as in recruitment, is the online and digital space, some institutions polled use some form of social media as part of their marketing and overall operations to build excellent teaching quality image. Websites often feature elements, including navigation bars, engaging visuals, such as slide how and prominent " call to actions" that encourage students to apply for examples.

How can new technology influence to change teaching method to raise better teaching quality? Newer methods of online and technology enhanced course delivery, including flipped classrooms and instruction model in particular have resulted in greater student engagement. Adaptive learning technology has also enjoyed significant interest and new technologies are currently under development by Fujitsu, MIT and the Apolle Group.

As universities find the ever increasing and diverse student base, so successful branding can help with increasing enrollment, expanding fundraising capabilities and other outcomes, e.g. building excellent teaching quality image. Teaching technological method includes, responsive website design can be viewed on multiple devices and platforms; searching engine optimization, e.g. Google can be used to research new teaching programs particularly, colleague and universities can rely on data driven analytics to determine who, how, and where which are reaching audiences from web analytical software to gather students age, sex, choice, countries, client segments judge how to achieve teaching method strategies more easy from online technology.

It seems that the university would build better teaching quality image if it had better communication method with students. Because online communications can be committed to maintaining and improving teaching quality by gather facts data and evidence, such as rankings, accreditations, applicant data (number and quality), recruitment of professors, placement of graduates agreement with partners, media presence, anything that demonstrate the teaching quality, as the excellence of the institution helps and strengthens of its brand. It seems digital technology can assist any universities to build excellent teaching quality image more easily.

Can universities innovate its courses content to raise lecturers' teaching quality? For example, health and medicine, energy security and efficiency, education and defense and homeland security etc. high technologic subjects. Has it relationship between teaching quality and course content? I feel that attractive course content can influence individual lecturer to choose how to teach whose students to make them to raise enjoyable feeling more easily. So, research universities must need to improve management, productivity and cost efficiency in both administration and academics because young faculty have insufficient opportunities to launch academic courses and research programs. If universities hope students have more interesting to choose to study those subjects Doctoral and Postdoctoral preparation could be enhanced by shortenng time to degree, raising completion rated and enhancing programs' effectiveness in providing training for highly productive careers.

A recognition of the importance of supporting the comprehensive nature of the research university, academic and professional disciplines, including the physical, the arts and humanities courses innovation to enable universities to provide the research and education programs required by a knowledge and innovation-driven global economy. The nation's research universities should set and achieve goals in cost containment efficiency and productivity in business operations and academic programs innovation to attract students to have more courses interesting to choose to study those courses. Hence, internet learning and promotion methods can assist universities to reduce expenditures if which can build the excellent teaching quality image for long term. As, the traditional suppliers of higher education, universities today are operating in a rapidly changing environment. As well as coping with less resources, traditional learning (teaching) has evolved: access to information is now freely available online; with smart phones, mobile to learn. It changes the student individual habits and expectations. New online models represent a real opportunity to improve access to higher education. For example, demographic changes are opening up global opportunities for universities and new education producers. In Asia, many students need high quality education, such as China and India students have the need for new models for delivering education.

Limited public resources and information and knowledge now will freely available online, the old system of broad-based learning, institutional research and a large in house support staff is being shaken up. The market for online learning needs had been increasing every year. Asia's online degree program is growing at a rate of 17.3% faster than anywhere in the world. Seven out of the top 10 countries with the highest e-learning growth rates in the world are in Asia. It seems Asia will be the popular new online education market. Moreover, many universities are also starting to offer more model of learning, students are taught using a mixture of online learning and face-to-face fuition rather than solely through traditional lecturing. It seems online and face-to-face education method will have chance to raise teaching quality among either only face-to-face classroom or only online education method. So it seems that teaching method can influence teaching quality. We can't rely on delivering content anywhere, it is all about contextualization ways of thinking and the student experience. Traditionally, universities hold key to knowledge in both a physical and philosophical sense. University libraries faculty and research institutes were where knowledge was created, stored and shared. Now, students hope to absorb knowledge with a device and connectivity, not just facts and figures, but also analysis and interpretation.

Today, access is expanding both in developed markets, such as Australia and even more fundamentally in China's tertitary education market. As China education participation rate had raised from 8% to 25.9% in the first decade of this century, and is likely to double again in the next 10 to 15 years. For universities, this will drive new approaches to teaching and learning create opportunities for entry to new innovating education markets and new low cost distribution in area, for quality of education needs. For example, digital technologies won't cause the disappearance of the campus-based university. Campuses will exist as places of teaching and learning, research, community engagement and raised forms of student experience. Assuming universities can deliver a rich, on campus experience. But, digital technology will transform the way education is delivered and supported, for example, through applications that enable real time student feedback, the way education is accessed in remote and regional areas, both in the developed and developing world.

Online teaching can provide attractive image to let science students to raise learning more interesting. How does learning about scientists during their scientific knowledge building affect students' science learning? For example, a control group in which students main learned information about the physic contents, who were studying how to increase students' interest in physical lessons, recall of science concepts, and physical problem solving. How can lecturer help scientific subject students create perceptions of scientists at hardworking individuals to make scientific progress? In addition, it also increased their delayed recall of the key science concepts and improved their abilities to solve complex problems. So, any lecturer needs to provide an opportunity for students to relate scientists to their knowledge-building activities has important implications for science learning and instruction. How does lecturer increase efforts to students' motivation to learn by creating instructional materials , e.g. textbooks or computer-based instructional materials that are more interesting, fun, or engaging for students ? For instance, many science text-books incorporate stimulating illustrations or visual images are in order to motivate students to learn the context. Another common approach to increase motivation is to promote students' interest in science by enhancing the overall reability of the texts. The efforts are undoubtedly important for science education as textbooks.

Goal setting raises teaching quality challenge

How to set goal to motivate and to educate science subject students more easily? Some education professionals (educators) had encouraged how to use effort belief to motivate students' learning, particularly in the area of science education is to use stories that illustrate scientists' stuggles toward new discoveries. Many science educators have suggested that a scientist's personal narratives, anecdote, self-reflections or life stories are valuable resources to inspire science learning (Eshach, 2009; Haven, 2007;Klopter, 199; Martin & Brouwer, 1991, 1993; McKinney & Michalovic, 2004; Milne, 1998; Rowcliffe, 2004; Solomon, 2002; Stinner, 1995; Stinner & Williams, 1993). So, it seems that any educator ought depend on the subject's unique feature or characteristics to decide how to teach whose students. So, teaching science subject, the educator needs to give himself/herself life story, self reflections in order to raise the subject's attraction and whose students' interesting to learn the science subject. Because a scientist's intellectual, personal and social struggles that led to important inventions and discoveries, if the educator can give personal life experience to let students to feel how who can encounter science to whose daily life. Then, it is possible that the educator's personal life experience can lead whose students to create important inventions and discoveries during who will become scientists in the future.

In special, the science educators also need to design of an online learning environment to provide to whose students to explore science at their own pace and in their spare time. Therefore, all of the self study activities took place in an online learning environment. One main reason for this design was high speed internet access, but lacked meaningful online learning resources. The informal online learning environment was designed to serve as a resource to supplement the school's formal science instruction. Also the online lessons consisted of the following two components: the first is science content, consisting of the physical lessons described above, and the second is achievement oriented stories about the scientists, including the image of the scientists and their personal backgrounds. It aims to raise students' interest in science research.

Why do higher education need to raise teaching quality? For India higher education needs example, India has a low rate of the supply and demand enrolment gap nowadays, at only 18%, compared with 26% in China and 36% in Brazil. There is unmet demand for higher education. The reason is the low quality of teaching and learning is providing to India's higher education system. The system is beset by issues of quality in many of its institutions, a shortage of faculty, poor quality teaching, outdated and lack of accountability and quality assurance and separation of research and teaching. With a very low level of PHD enrolment, India doesn't have enough high quality researchers, there are few opportunities for interdisciplinary and multidisciplinary working, lack of early stage research experience, a weak ecosystem for innovation and low levels of education industry engagement in India education system. So, India education institutions are facing challenges to influence the low enrolment rate. Although, India's population is growing, but it's higher education student numbers is decreasing. I believe the factor causing is main source from the poor lacking quality. Hence, India educators need to spend more time to research how to improve their educational methods to attract many students to enroll to universities to study.

Goal setting is one important factor to influence the country's education system or the school's teaching method succeed whether it can success or fail to improve its teaching quality. Goal setting is the process of establishing an outcome (a goal) to serve as the aim of one's actions. In educational settings, the ultimate outcome is usually some form of learning as operationalized by the instructor and/or the students (Marzano, Pickering, & Pollock, 2001, p.93).

Setting goals can be specially important for students with low achievement motivation. In an experimental study, authors identified college students as having either high or low achievement motivation. Students in each group, were then randomly placed into either goal setting group where they decided how may anagram who would solve or into the control groups (Horn & Murphy, 1985). The research result indicated that when students with high achievement motivation performed equally well in both goal conditions, self-set goals enhanced the performances of students with low achievement, motivation. Therefore, instructors may encourage students to set goals if whose motivation to achieve is low.

How schools can set goals and what schools make a good goal to which student. The most important step toward goal attainment is to set effective goals. There are many factors that influence the effectiveness. Studies have documented that individuals with clear, written goals are significantly more likely to succeed. Then, whose without clearly defined goals. In a study conducted by Ferguson and Sheldon (2010), participants write " why and how" who will achieve a goal. There was an interaction between the level of initial goal-relevant skills and the effectiveness of writing "why or how" of the goals. Students with initially low goal-relevant skills were more likely to internalize their goals over time and report greater goal expectancies of who wrote about the "how" of the goals. Therefore, education ought not neglect to encourage whose students to attract to write what whose goals are and explain why there are their goals and how to plan to achieve their goals. It aims to build their confidence to know why who choose to study the subject and how who need to study the subject to achieve their study plan successfully. So, procedural written goals are strategies that students may use to achieve a goal, such as learning a problem solving strategy. For example, outcomes goals strategies are specific to an activity at hand, such a solving fraction problems or writing an essay on specific procedure and outcome goals on students' motivation, learning and self-efficacy. Suchunk and Rice (1991) found that the best way to promote self-efficacy and achievement is to couple the process goal with progress feedback on well the students use a strategy.

Why educators need to encourage students to set whose goals to learn in their learning process. Because students need to know their progress toward their goals, especially when working an accomplishing procedure goals. Also instructors can give feedback that stresses processes, such as how well student are using a strategy, budgeting their time, and completing sub-goals. When instructors implement outcome goals, who may consider giving students feedback on how well who are doing currently compared with low who did previously. Such comparisons would raise student self-efficacy, ultimately, student should learn to monitor their goals and analyze the progress made toward attaining them. So, written setting goals is a learning progress to let students to write to remember what whose goals planning are and to remember why these are whose goals and to remember how who plan to achieve whose goals in their learning process. If who forget what are whose goals or sub-goals and /or how to achieve their goals or sub-goals and/or why these are their goals or sub-goals in their learning process any time. Then, who can take their written note to remember again and to revise whether who can improve their ability to achieve their goals or sub-goals in any stage during their learning process. Till to the end of the course, who can revise what the factors are caused to their failure to get poor grade and how to avoid solve the challenges will be caused in next time learning process. Hence, goal setting is a good educational psychological method to prepare to choose the best educational method and course content and to build/raise students' confidence to learn more easily during whose learning process in schools. I suggest educators ought use this education method to let whose students to attempt to practice in any course beginning.

Teaching contents and class room management challenge

I think content knowledge can be a barrier to teacher development. The problem is when the education content becomes the be-all and end-all of the teaching process. When the content matters more than anything. When course content is that important, faculty are prevented from using methods that enhance how much students learn. In this case, the educational course content orientation of faculty hurts students and teachers in possible.

When teachers think the only, the best, the most important way to improve their teaching is by developing their content knowledge, who neglect to consider the teaching contents levels of knowledge, but who have only simplistic instructional methods to convey that teaching material. Both are essential what teachers teach and how who teach it are linked and very much dependent on one another.

Even though both are tightly linked, which are still separate. Development of one doesn't automatically improve how the other functions. So teachers can work to grow teaching content knowledge, but if the methods used to convey that knowledge are not sophisticated, teaching may still be quite ineffective. It may not motivate students efficient, as well as it may not result in more and better student learning. Because teachers only feel whose teaching content most the best educational quality.

The typical college teacher has spent years in courses developing the knowledge still set and virtually no time on the teaching set. This way of preparing professors assumes that the content is much more complex than the process, when in fact both are not equally fair to treat. The teaching content and the process requires the best knowledge level to be prepared to teachers to teach. Some kinds of contents are the best taught by example, some by experience. Other kinds are the best understood when discussed and worked on other kinds need individual reflection and analysis. Besides these learning and teaching both demands of the content itself, there are the learning needs of individual student.

The best teachers are not always, no even usually, those teachers with the most sophisticated content knowledge. The best teachers ought know their teaching material, but who also ought know a lot about the teaching process. They follow themselves instructional methods, teaching strategies and approaches, just as whose content knowledge develops. They never underestimate the power of the teaching process to determine the outcome. With this understanding, content is not a barrier to teacher development.

How to identify effective teaching methods for the large class environment? What teaching methods are effective in the large class environment? What are students' perceptions of these methods? In common, used teaching methods include lecture, discussion, combination, case study, team project which were applied and evaluated in a large class setting. In addition, improvement on student feelings about large versus small classes and student opinions of the teaching methods was gathered.

Large class environment is needed to offer strategies for course design, student engagement, active learning and assessment. The advantage of large classes include decreased instructor costs, efficienct use of faculty time and talent , availability of resources and standardization of the learning experence. But, there are significant disadvantages to large class teaching environment including impersonal relations between students and the instructor, limited range of teaching methods, discomfort among instructors teaching large classes.

Has it relationship between class size and student performance to influence teaching quality. The traditional passive view of learning involves situations where material is delivered to students using a lecture based format. In contrast, a more modern view of learning is constructivism, where students are expected to be active in the learning process by participating in discussion and/or collaborative activities (Fosnot, 1989). Some educational professionals suggested that lecture leaded to the ability to recall facts, but discussion produced higher level comprehension. Further, research on group-oriented discussion methods had shown that team learning and student-led discussions didn't only produced favorable student performance outcomes, but also raised greater student participation in large class. In terms of students' preferences for teaching methods, a study by Qualters (2001) suggests that "students do not favor active learning methods because of the in-class time taken by the activities, fear of not covering all of the material in the course, and anxiety about changing from traditional classroom expectations to the active structure". I suggest that lecturers can assess of the course, preferences for class size to decide perceptions of teaching methods. Students were asked a series of questions to gather information on their perceptions of the course, as well as their preferences for class size 89% of respondents indicated that the course has been of value to them, likewise 90% of respondents indicated that who had learned a lot in the course and 86% rated. The topic material is interesting. 51% of respondents indicated a preference for small class sizes less than 50 students .

Effective management of large classes is a popular topic among faculty in higher education, it is possible that universities feel which will influence lecturers' teaching quality to satisfy student's individual learning needs. However, some surveys indicated that 99% of respondents reported that who were currently enrolled in large classes generally. However, the surveys' result could conclude that these teaching methods were accepted positively to affect student's individual learning needs. Students scores improved most under the jigsaw method, and least under the team project method, whereas the lecture, lecture/discussions and case study methods produced similar improvement. The finding suggested that moderately active learning methods, such as the jigsaw method is more effective than the lecture, lecture/discussions and case study method. However, more extreme active learning methods, such as team projects completed outside of class may not be as effective as moderately -active or passive teaching method.

The findings of the study also demonstrate that most students (51%) have a preference for small class sizes (less than 50 students). However, some students (38%) indicated no preference for class size, when the remaining 10% indicated a preference for large classes 100 or more large classes. So, it implied that most students did not like large class environment to study. However, the finding indicated the lecture/ discussion teaching method was the most preferred among students. Students commented as to their reason for selecting this as the most valuable method who have a desire to be an action learners engaging in discussion rather than passively listening to a lecture.

Measuring teacher effectiveness challenge

Can measure teacher effectiveness to judge whether the teacher individual teaching quality is achieved to the minimum requirement? Generally, on Asia countries, teachers need even more sophistic abilities to teach more complex educational resources at home, who are new English language learners, and those who have distinctive learning needs.

In recent years, there has been growing interest in moving beyond traditional measures of teacher qualifications, such as completion of a preparation program, number of degrees, or years of experience, in order to evaluate teachers' actual performance as the basic for making decision about hiring. How should we measures teacher effective? So, how to judge whether the teaching quality is achieved to the minimum requirement, for nursing engineering, accounting, medicine and other skilled professions etc. subjects.

Why do teachers need performance assessment to raise teaching quality? How well teachers have developed the classroom teaching skills to be effective with their students, a graduate's commitment to teaching as a professional career, feedback from graduates and employers and high quality tests of their knowledge and skills that are tied to classroom teaching performance. I believe that new assessments are needs to tell whether teacher education graduated have developed the classroom teaching skills to be effective with their students because current teacher tests don't directly measure what teachers do in the classroom, and who don't indicate how well teachers will do in the classroom.

In nearly all states, teachers have to pass at least three tests, generally multiple choice tests of basic skills, subject matter and teaching knowledge, in order to become licensed, even though these are not strongly related to their ultimate success in the classroom. Furthermore, in many cases these tests evaluate teacher knowledge before who enter or complete teacher education, and hence are an inadequate tool for teacher education accountability.

Performance assessment aims to measure what teachers actually do in the classroom, and which have been to be related to later teacher effectiveness. So, this method has potential to raise teaching quality in possible. It can be a value added method for examining student learning gains into teacher evaluation. As Harvard University economics professor Thomas Kane pointed out in recent senate testimony, these measures have been subject to concerns about their ability at the individual teacher level and the possibility who could teach toward narrow tests, as well as the fact, who are not available for about three-fourths of all teachers. So, whose observational measures is due to the fact that the sore gains measure more than the influence of the teacher, even when statistical methods are used to control for other factors, such as student characteristics, home and school resources and the influence of other teachers, tutors, and parents on learning. Furthermore, also most expectation agree that at least three years of data about a given teacher are necessary to achieve a stability, the direct use of student test score data to evaluate teachers doesn't help inform judgements about new entrants to the education profession.

However, I commend that how certain kinds of classroom observations and videotapes of teaching, teacher reflect, context pedagogical assessments and student and teacher feedback can be related to measures of teacher effectiveness, based on student achievement gains on both traditional tests and more intellectually challenging open-ended measures. These methods can raise teaching quality indirectly. Thus, effort to create more consistency in evaluating teacher performance are critical if performance is to be a central measure of teacher effectiveness.

Relationship challenge between teacher and students to high quality of teaching

Can teacher and peer relationships on students' classroom engagement and motivation influence teaching quality as individual teacher? I believe that the quality of student's relationships with teacher and peer is a fundamental substrate for the development of academic engagement and achievement and it can influence teaching quality. It is easy to think students are learning forward in their seats, hands waving, questions and opinions rolls out, offering the teacher a clear picture of what students understand and where confusion remains. Students like to attempt groups learning and continue discussions, showing their comprehension through questions, critical listening and arguing about examples, who apply the material to whose own lives . The teacher is thoroughly energized, thinking about how the material to be covered next builds on that day's class.

Student engagement and motivation are precious commodities, valuable not only to teachers but also to students. Students school lives are more enjoyable when who are engaged in their classes. I think student intrinsic motivation is a factor which can influence whose learning ability from the teacher's teaching . So the teacher's teaching behavior is a extrinsic motivation to excite whose students to feel whose teaching quality level is high or low (satisfactory or non satisfactory). The caring teacher and student relationships and high quality peer relationships for student academic self-perceptions, school engagement, motivation, learning and teaching performance, which does close influence. Teachers and students recognize high quality relationships , who seem effortless because who are intrinsically motivating, enjoyable and mutually reinforcing. Teachers and students also know when relationships are not working, and unfortunately, such relationships are also self-sustaining in ways that detract from instruction and erode classroom cohesion. To support teachers in meeting this challenge.

I shall attempt to explain why classroom relationships work and don't work and to offer practical strategies to help teachers to improve the motivational dynamics of difficult relationships. The bottom line is that teachers are forced to spend more time engaged in activities who feel compete with good teaching. It is easy to imagine high quality relationships in the classroom. Interactions are courteous and kind, and who focus on learning them material and building academic skills ; students provide constructive criticism and are receptive to feedback, the classroom is welcoming but focused on academics.

Why do these relationships work? An useful way of explaining the complex dynamics of relationships is through the motivational model. To raise teaching quality to let students to feel teachers need provide structured interactions in which teaches need set high standards, clear expectations and reasonable limits for students' behaviors and performance and consistently follow through on their demands. Optimal structure includes teachers' confidence in students' abilities as well as help students figure out how to reach high levels of understanding and performance.

Finally, teachers' autonomy support shapes student motivation , when teachers treat students with respect and seek out, listen to and value their opinions. Therefore, it has good relationship between the teacher and whose students. Then, students feel who are considered and feel the teacher can provide good educational (teaching) quality as the same time . So, every teacher needs consideration to student's engagement of emotion.

Why has it close relationship between raising teaching quality and the teacher is effective ? There is only one way to obtain student achievement and the research is very specific. It is the teacher and what the teacher knows and can do that is the determining factor with student achievement. Any students will learn based on whether the teacher is effective or ineffective. I feel that district variables don't matter; school variables don't matter; program variables don't matter; It is the teacher that matter. Because the ineffective teachers get poor results. Otherwise, the effective teachers get good results and it makes no difference to the good teacher. What teachers give whose students. What programs who teach them and who the administrators are. The bottom line is that there is one way to create good schools, without good teachers as well as it is the administrator who creates a good school and it is the teacher who creates a good school and it is the teacher who creates a good classroom.

Is shortage of good teaching discipline relationship not provide good quality of teaching ? It is really quite simple to solve this challenge. Institutions can fix leak by providing adequate training and support for beginning teachers (known as indication), thereby, increasing the retention of more competent, qualified and satisfied professionals for classrooms. Due to the reason, teacher is the only factor that can improve student achievement. The major problem of lack of procedures and routines and discipline can influence the quality of teaching. So, if the school had good classroom management skills, then it can substantially improve student achievement. Therefore, effective classroom management skill can cause effective teaching, then effective teaching can raise good quality of teaching to let students to enjoy learning benefits form the teachers.

I shall indicate these three questions: What is quality teaching and why it is important in higher education? How can teaching concretely be enhanced? How can one make sure quality teaching initiatives are effective?

Nowadays, quality teaching has become an issue of important changing, increased interactive competition, increasing social and geographical diversity of the student body, increasing demands of value for money, introduction of information techniques etc. Quality teaching initiatives are very diverse both in nature and in function. However, research points out that quality teaching is necessarily student-centered. It's aim is most and all student learning. Thus, attention should be given simply to the teacher's opinion of teaching.

Quality teaching has become an issues of importance to higher education. The student body has considerably expanded and diversified, both socially and geographically. New students call for new teaching methods. Modern technologies have entered the classroom, thus modifying the nature of the interactions between students and professors. The governments, the students and their families, the employers, the fund providers increasingly demand value for their money and desire more efficiency through teaching. In fact, conceptions of quality teaching happen to be stakeholder relative : students, teachers or evaluation agencies don't share the definition what good teaching or good teacher is. In general, good teachers have empathy for students, who are generally experienced teachers and most of all who are generally experienced teachers and most of all who are organized and expensive, those who have passions: passions for learnings for their field, for teaching and for their students. But research also demonstrates that good teaching depends on what is being taught and on other situational factor. Some research -centered, it's aim is most and for all student learning. Thus, attention should be given not simply to the teacher's teaching skills, but also to the learning environment that must address the student's personal needs: students should know why who are working, should be also to relate to other students and to receive help if needed. Adequate support to staff and students (financial support, social and academic support, support to minority students services etc.), also improves learning outcomes. So, groups of students and/or teachers who need learn and build knowledge through intellectual interaction, are judged to enhance on student learning by increasing students' and teachers' satisfaction.

How can teaching be enhanced to raise quality? Quality teaching initiatives are very diverse both in nature and in function. The most currently used quality initiatives seem to aim to enhance teamwork between teachers, goal-setting and course plans. However, gathering information and reading the literature, are looking outside the classrooms, are important fools to improve quality of teaching, but who are still under-employed. Another point to keep in mind, how to enhance student learning. The focus of quality teaching initiatives should not always be on the teacher. Rather it should encompass the whole institution and the learning environment. Another of major drivers for enhancemnt of quality teaching concerns teachers' leadership. However the role of the department, of the educational support divisions and that of the central university, which can value quality culture part of its mission statement are central.

How can school make sure quality teaching is effective? I recommend that it is essential to measure the impact of the quality teaching initiatives in order to be able to improve these initiatives. However, assessing the quality of one's teaching remains challenging. The choice of indicators to measure quality teaching is important, because it has been shown that assessment drive-learning, how the teacher is judged with undoubtedly impact whose teaching methods. Indicators to access the quality of teaching (the value of graduates, satisfaction of teachers, retention rates etc.) of an institution proved of case but carry various meanings and even lead to misunderstandings. Researchers agree that reliable indicators should be chosen, and not just the most practical ones. Moreover, classroom management skills should be discussed for teacher's individual method how to influence quality of teaching.

Assessing the results of quality teaching initiatives has proven to be difficult, and this issue has received increasing attention in the literature. What are the experiences, purposes and methods to support quality teaching? What are the major drivers that support quality teaching and the factors that hinder quality teaching? How traditional and innovative methods are used to assess and improve quality teaching initiatives? In fact, the difficulties may teachers in higher education are encountered with when assessing the impact of those initiatives that are meant to enhance the quality of teaching. The fact that a great proportion of studies on quality teaching were carried out on a very limited scale (specifically concerned with a small group of students or specific disciplines of study).

What is quality teaching and why is it important in higher education? How can teaching be enhanced? How can one make sure quality teaching initiative are effective? I shall force on teaching inputs and learning outcomes. Instead of focusing simply on the question of what a good teacher is, I feel that a good or excellent teacher may indeed help whose students, but whose contribution to the field of teaching will be weak if who does not share whose discoveries with whose colleagues or analyze whose own methods. Also I believe the quality of learning environment can be improved if teaching should be both research-formed and research driven.

Nowadays, students are therefore very concerned about the quality of the lecturers who pay for. Next, the internet has globalized the market place, and the institutions are increasingly competing for the best students, nationally international students, and consequently may develop now teaching strategies. Teaching methods concern aspects of online learning need to become familiar with new teaching methods. Distance education in print form is being supplemented by internet, based delivery. Mixed modes of learning have become common: the majority of cross border distance program now involves some form of face-to-face or administrator contact, sometimes visits to study centers. Generally people in remote locations and working adults are the student role to attempt this new form of learning. As globalization continues, the international competition for the best students is likely to increase among higher education institutions, thus among reinforcing pressure for quality teaching. It is likely that international rankings based on the quality of teaching will be attractive of quality initiatives.

Harvey and Green (1993) distinguish four definitions of quality that can help us to understand what quality teaching might be. First, quality is as excellence, the traditional conception of quality is the dominant one. Second, quality can be defined as value for money, a quality institution in this is one that satisfies the demands of public accountability. Third, quality may seen as fitness for purpose, the purpose being that of the students to learn sciences efficiently. The last, definition explained quality as transforming, it means quality teaching is teaching that transforms students' perceptions and the way who go about applying their knowledge to real world problems . Quality assurance in higher education has also become a focus of attention for private universities. Students who are increasingly paying tuition fee might now be considered as clients of higher education institutions. It caused that students are also my concerned about the quality of lectures who pay for. As the culture of higher education has become increasingly market-oriented and external demands for quality of teaching have increased.

Teaching methods have also changed. Professors who wish to use online education method to teach students. Because of all these changes, several questions has been caused: can the possessive of a PHD be taken as a proxy for teaching competence? What constitutes good and approriate teaching? How can a quality culture in higher education, that supports quality teaching be defined and achieved? Dickinson et al. (1995) point out that " education may be unique in the sense that it is difficult for the client to assess the quality and relevance of the service (p.63).

In fact, it sometimes happens that only years after an university course, a student at least comes to understand why this particular courses was useful. Another side, some educators identified quality culture was based on two distinct elements: a set of value, belief, expectations and commitment towards quality, a structural/managerial element with well defined processes that enhance quality and coordinate effects. However, it has relationship between quality teaching and quality culture relationship. Because every classroom has different learning culture, learning environment, teaching performance, teaching resources, educational time spending, learning of satisfaction level. So, educators need to understand whose classroom and students culture, then, who may have more ability to understand how to teach whose students in the classroom more easily.

The role and status accorded to teachers is being reassessed increase. Indeed, it is easy to understand that the quality of its teachers. But in order to enhance and reward teaching excellence, it is essential to know what constitutes good teaching. Good teaching depends on whom and what is being taught. It concerns between student entry characteristics and effective teaching behaviors. In general, content-unfamiliar students' perception of learning is more positively influenced by the professor's organization than by the professor's expressiveness. However, students who are familiar with the course content are more sensitive to the professor's expressiveness than to whose organization skill.

In conclusion, student individual learning emotion and educational environment and teacher individual teaching method and classroom management and their relationship and learning and teaching culture these factors can influence overall quality of teaching to any higher education institutions.

Reference

Armstrong & Kotler, P.(2007).Marketing on introduction (8th ed.), Upper Saddle River, New Jersey: Person Education, Inc.

Dickinson, K.D. Pollock, A, & Troy, J. (1995), " perceptions of the value of quality assessment in scottis higher education", Assessment and evaluation in higher education, vol. 20, no 1, pp. 59-66.

Ellwood, D.T. and T.J. kane (2000). Who is getting a college education? Family background and growing gaps in enrollment. In securing the future investing in children from birth to college, eds. S. Daneiger and J. Waldfoges 283-324. New York: Russe Sage Foundation.

Eshach, H. (2009). The Nobel Prize In The Physics Class: Science, history and glamour. Science & Education, 18, 1377-1393. doi: 10.1007/s 11191-008-9172-4.

Ferguson, Y., & Sheldon, K.M. (2010). Should goal strivers, think about "why " or "how" to strive? It depends on their skill level. Motivation and emotion 34-253-265.

Fosnot, C. (1989). Enquiring teachers, enquiring learners. New York: Teachers college press.

Harvey, L. & Green, D. (1993) " Defining quality",
Assessment and evaluation in higher education,
vol, 18, pp.8-35.

Horn, H.L. & Murphy, M.D. (1985). Low need achievers' performance: The positive impact of
a self-determined goal. Personality and social
psychology Bulletin, 11, 275-285.

Huang, H.I. (2012). An empirical analysis of the strategic
Management of competitive advantage: a case
study of higher technical and vocational education
in Taiwan (Doctoral dissertation,
Victoria University).

Kim, Y. J., and J.W. Lee 2009. Technological Change, Human Capital Structure and Multiple Growth Paths, ADB Economics Working Paper Series No. 149, Economics And Research Dept. Asian Development Bank, Manila.

Marzano, R.J., Pickering, D.J., & Pollock, J.E. (2001). Classroom instruction that works.
Alexandria, VA: ASCD.

Qualters, D. (2001). Do students want to be active?
The Journal of job.

Schunk, D.H., & Rice, J.M. (1991). Learning goals and progress feedback instruction. Journal of reading behavior. 23, 351-364.

Trigwell, K., Prosser, M. & Waterhouse, F. (1999)
Relations Between Teachers' Approaches To
Teaching And Students' Approaches To
LearningHigher Education 37: 57-70.

Universiti teknologi, MARA 2009, Key performance indicators (kpis, for governance of public universities in Malaysia, Shah Alam: Asian Centre for Research On University Learning and Teaching) ACRULET. Universiti, teknologi MARA.

Can educators apply what methods of
knowledge to solve problem

When one educator encounters any challenges concern education or non education aspects, how can he/she apply knowledge methods to attempt to solve problem from himself/herself? Hence, school management staffs do not need to spend time to make appointment to arrange small group meeting to discuss him/her problem, if the school has many teachers , they feel difficult to solve any problems, then the school often needs to waste other teachers and management staffs whose time and increases human resource number to make appointments for many time meetings to discuss their educational or personal problem often.

The long time frequent meetings will cause teachers feel poor nervous and influence poor teaching performance when they need to spend at least one hour overtime extra meeting time to do group members discussion several day, even every day per week. I shall explain some knowledge methods to let teachers can attempt to solve any education or non education challenges when they are encountering in schools.

Conceiving of social structure in school educational environment, it is as external to teaches themselves help them take its self-evident educational experience learning knowledge effects upon their daily teaching lives into themselve understanding of the social behavior. It seems that the teacher's one student' s learning attitude or learning activities, how and why he/she often does his/her behavior in school. So, the teacher can apply his/her daily educational experience to attempt to evaluate or final reasons or judge which factors can cause the student often does his/her team poor learning behavior or poor learning attitude in classroom.

How does the student often does poor refers to response either to externl environmental stimuli, (e.g. another student's learning behavior influence, or the demands of teacher's influence or to internal stimuli (feeling interest to learn if he/she feel achieve the examination pass to the subject, then he/she will hard to learn and listen the teacher's teaching the subject in classroom. This may be tought of as student individual learning behavior with meaning. It is the student's intentional learning behavior and as such, future oriented, e.g. good grade achievement aim, none any subjects fail aim, earning teacher's appreciation for his/her learning performance, comparison examination result to classmates etc. different future oriented aim.

A large number of students everyday interactions with one another rely on such shared learning experiences in every lesson. A student for example, raises his arm and keeps it above his head. Should he do this at home when watching televisions, his parents are likely to find his bodily movements (What's the matter with him? i.e. what immediate, past event cause him to behave like that?) In the setting of the classroom, however, the action is perfectly understandable, i.e. what does he intend? or alternatively, he is letting the teacher knows that he is ready to answer the teacher's question when he asks him , i.e. future oriented , intentional behavior. So, any teacher can attempt to observe why every student often does his/her same behavior in classroom. It is only two factors to influence he/she does the same behavior in classroom, it is either the student personal internal psychological factor or external environment factor both , they can influence the student often does the same behavior in classroom.

Hence, observation is one knowledge method to let every teacher can find how any why the student often does the same behavior in classroom, when the student often learns lazy or he/she often absent in classroom or performs poor learning behavior to influence classmates can listen what the teacher's speaking in classroom. All these poor learning behavior or attitude will have one or more either the student's personal internal psychological factor or external environment factor or both factors influence his/her poor learning behavioural performance in classroom. So, the teacher can observe the student's some behavioral perofrmance to evaluate whether his/her behavior is caused from himself/herself personal internal psychological factor or external environment factor or both factors influence hs/she often feel need to do the same poor learning behavior in classroom. For example, cultural differenc between students, it can influence the differcnt countries students' choice to do different learning behavior in classroom. When one clasroom has Asian and Western students are learning in classroom. In actually getting at the realities of the different cultural learning situation, they provide insights of day-for-day discrimination and offer a compelling account of the cultural processes by which pupils' responses to school are mediated. It is possible that when the Asian pupils , e.g. China, Japan, Hong Kong, Singapore etc. countries pupils, they has chose to study in the Western,e.g. US one oversea university to study. When the US studetns feel these different Asian countries' enrollment to influence some themselves US domestic pupils can not succeed to enrol this US university to study. However, these US doemstic university students can feel angry to all these Asian pupils' successful enrollment to cause their other US domestic students' learning choice to be lost to this university. So, these US domestic pupils will often do not polit or not friendly behavior to treat these any one of Asian countries' pupils in classroom. Also, the Asian countries' pupils will often do the same not polite or not unfriendly behavior to treat them in classrooom. It is possible that some Asian countries' they may be fear some US domestic pupils' not polite or not unfriendly behavior. So their absenteeism will be caused from these US domestic pupils' not polite or not friendly behavior influences .

So, the university US teacher can attempt consider this internal environment factor can influence how any why Asian and Western pupils, they often do the not polite and not friendly learning behaviours or learning attitude to influence their successful learning attitude in every lesson. Som cultural difference will be one possible influential factor to cause they choose to to the different learning attitude or behavior between Asian and Western pupils, when one school has the Asian and Western pupils , they need to often learn and contact in the cultural different learning environment.

I shall indicate the criteria for evaluating historical research to the different educational problems when the teacher is encountering. The educator can use quantitative method. It is by for the greater part of research in historical studies in qualitative in nature. This is because thr proper subject matter of historical research consists to a greater extent of verbal and other symbolic material from a society or a cultural's past. The basic skills requires of the educator to analyse this kind of qualitative or symbolic material involve collecting classifying, ordering, synthesizing, evaluating and interpreting.

At the basic of these arts lies personal judgement. In the comparatively recent past.

However, attempts have been made to apply quantitative methods of the scientist to the solution of historical problems or student poor learning behavioral performance or poor attitude problems of these methods , the one having greatest relevance to historical research is that of content analysis, the basic goal of which is to take a verbal , non-quantitative document and transform it into quantitative data.

I recommend that the educator can follow these steps to attempt to make any problems.

The first step is identification of the problem. Has the problem been clearly defined? It is difficult enough to conduct historical research adequately without adding to the confusion by starting out with an obvious major problem. Is the problem capable of solution? Is it within the competence of the investigator?

The second step is gathering data . Are data of a primary nature available in sufficient completeness to provide a solution , or has there been an overdependence on secondary or unverifiable sources?

The third step is Data analysis. Has the dependability dependability of the data been adequately established? Has the relevance of the data been adequately explored?

The fourth step is interpretation. Does the another teacher display adequate mastery of his data and insight into the relative significance for this teacher's problem solution in reference? Does the another teacher display adequate teaching experience, adequate teaching historical perspective or background for his personal problem solution in reference? Does the another teacher maintenance his objectivity or does he allow personal bias to distort this teacher personal problem encountering evidence? Are this teacher and another teacher themselves hypotheses are reasonable to be accepted or persuasive? Have they been adequately tested? Doed the encountering problem teacher see the relationship beteen his data and other historical similiar teaching problem encountering facts which had been ever occurred in the part?

The final idea is presentation. Does the style of problem solution writing attract as well as inform to persuade the school management staffs to believe? Does the report make a contribution on the basis of newly discovered data or new interpretation ? Does the teacher himself/herself recommendation to the problem solution reflect the actual problem situation that he/she is facing to be solved successfully?

For one interesting student learning behavioe research report example, Blatchford identifies interesting differences in attitudes between younger and older pupils and between subgroups differentiated by ethnicity and sex, data analysis in the research report. However, do not specifically deal with the views of the original sample of 133 children at ages seven and eleven . Because of the investigor avoids any speculation about causal relationships.

The research report indicates that at seven years of age, 42 per cent of the pupils found school "mostly interesting " when same 26 percent thought is " most boring". The same technique used at age seven to elicit children's views of school , a set of five faces ranging from a big smile, saying, "Great! . I love it" , it was employed again at age eleven . At that time, 58 per cent of the choldren chose the smiling face to register their feeling at the end of their junior school days, only 5 per cent expressing strong distaste choldren's attitudes towards maths is of particular interest. At seven years of age maths was the most popular subject , 71 per cent choosing one or the other of the smiling facces to express their approved . At eleven years of age, 75 per cent agsin chose one or other of their rating of maths. Asked why they felt like that about maths, the most common explanation was that maths was more interesting or more fun, they feel maths can persuade or encourage their brain working, enjoy problem solving and finding answers.

The investigators report sex and ethic differences. The most obvious of which, in their view, concerned the popularity of maths among the black boys. Black boys were far more likely to nominate maths as their favourite subject and to say they loved it. Morevoer, more said they liked maths because they are better at it. These may seem encouraging findings, observes. Blatchfords until one looks at achievement results obtained from the same children at the same time (Plewis, 1991).

So, it explains how any why many pupils like maths subject. Their internal personal psychologicl factor will be more influential to compare the external environment factor to influence they can raise interesting to learn maths. Also, it is possible that black boy pupils can feel more brains enjoyable feeling is encouraged by learning maths subject calculation or analysis processing. So, there are many black boy pupils enjoy to learn maths subject in the school. It concludes that the school's teacher can attempt to gather data to find why some pupils do not like learn maths, whether they dislike to learn maths, due to their boring teaching method or themselves psychological feeling.

However, in some situations, in fact, teachers ought not find any solutions to encountering edicational problem by themselve more easily. I shall indicate these sample situations examples, e.g. it can make more better decision concerns that staff room discussions of assessment featured more prominently, discussons became more critical , academic, analytical, reflective than one teacher personal data gathering methos, interviews need to revealed changes over time in the extent to which teachers and management staffs were informed and anger to discuss educational reforming issues to the school's long term education stategy, staff appointments to discusson brought a more reasonable or irrational acceptance view to evaluate themselve teaching performance, staff meeting agenda and the time devoted to certain issues revealed changes of focus, teaching quality of all teachers' cooperation interactions and debate suggested how to improve their teaching performance to be better, inquiries were made to the educator or researcher about university courses and applications for advanced diploma/master degree or doctural degree university courses, teaching contents and enrollment requirements to enrolling students. The acting headteacher's liaisons with other schools including piloting records of achievements and assessment innovations, changes in role orientation and the stress level of the headteacher, the head's emphasis on reassuring whose teaching staffs.

Hence, all these any one of educational problem(s) that is / are not easier to find the solutions from one teacher's data gathering method. Otherwise , a group management staffs and teachers meeting can find the more reasonable or irrational acceptance solutions to solve any one of those problems more easily because many educators can devote time to give themselves different unique personal opinions to evaluate whether whom opinion ought be chose to make the most reasonable or irrational judgement to decide whether which opinion is the best method to solve the problem more accurate. Hence, it means that none of all educating problems can be found the best solutions by the teacher himself/herself. Some of educating problems are needed to all teachers and management staffs appoint one long time meeting to discuss when opinion(s) is (are) the best solution(s).

However, some educational problems are needed to spend long time is devoted by teachers , after meeting. It is one experimental research. The steps include as below:

First, the researcher must identify and define th research problem as precisely as possible, always supporting that the problem is followed by experimental methods. Second, the researchers must formulate hypotheses that he/she wished to test. This involves making predictions about relationships between specific variables at the same time making decisions about other vriables that are to be excluded from the experiment by means of controls, variable remember. They have two properties. First, they must be measurable, psysical fitness, for example is not directly measurable until it has been operationally defined. Making the vaiable " physical fitness" operational means simply defining it by letting something else that is measurable for it, gymnastics test , perhaps. Second, the proxy variable must be a valid indicator of the hypothetical variable in which one is interested. That is to say, a gymnastics test probably is a reasonable proxy for physical fitness. Thirs, the researcher must selct appropriate levels at which to test th indepedent variables. By way of example, suppose an educational psychologist wishes to find out whether longer or shorter periods of reading setting. The educational psychologist will hardly select 5 hour and 5 minute periods and appropriate levels rather, he/she is more likely to choose 30 minute and 60 minute levels, in order to compare with usual timetabled periods of 45 minutes duration.

In other words, the experimentation will vary the stimuli at such levels as one of practical interest in the real-life situation, such as the teacher himself/herself actual teaching situational experience or actual be student learning situational experience in whose past educational career experience, pursuing the example of reading attatinment somewhat further, the hypothetical educating experiments will be wise to vary the stimuli, in large enough intervals so as to obtain measurable results. Comparing reading periods of between the 44 minutes and 46 minutes, or 50 minutes and 52 minutes with timetables reading lessons of 45 minutes or 51 minutes is scarcely likely to result in observable differences in attainment.

Fourth, in planning the design of the experiment, the educating researcher must take account of the sample pupils population to which he/she wishes to generalize his/her results more irrational or reasonable or accurate. This involves his/her decisions over sample sizes and sampling methods. Samplying decisions are bound up with questions of funds manpower and the amount of time available for experimentation.

Fifth, with problems of validity in mins, the researcher must select instruments, choose tests and decide upon and morale and is thus concerned with efficiency. Their motivations, relationships and teaching employee perfrmance problems, focuses on job analysis and aims at improving professional teaching functioning and efficiency, and teaching performance . It is concerned with the school itself organizational change, or as it results in improved functioning in educational industry or the school's teaching business problem, it is concerned with planning and policy making, innovation and change and the ways in which these may be implemented in ongoing educational systems, concentrates on special problem solving, provides the opportunity to develop theoretical knowledge, the emphasis being more on the research element of the method.

Hence, action research is only suitable to be applied to solve the special problems concern individual performance or improving efficiency or teaching quality or changing the school organization's long term educational strategic aims or policies issues. It does not solve any problems concern student emotion negative changing or poor learning behaviors or pooe learning attitudes to the behavioral issues, when the teacher is encountering any learning behavioral issues in classrooms.

However, the action resesearch is needed that the good relationship is built between all collaborative group participants be symmetrical , that the practice related to research tasks within the group be owned by the teacher researchers, that during the research project's life any of the participatns in the group may raise significant questons as to the direction the project may take, that the exchange of information between particpants is negotiated and controlled by the participants concerned, and that the roles of teacher, researcher are available to learner and all participants.

Moreover, all teachers need in possess certain skills which can contribute to the researched task . The important matter is to clarify and define one's own particular set of skills some teachers for example, are able to collect and interpret statistical data, others record any key variable information moments of a lesson. One teacher may know something about questionnaire design, another have a natural personal effort for interviewing . It is essential that teachers work from their own particular strengths when developing the research.

The situations within which teachers work impose different kinds of constraints. Some schooles , for example, are equipped with the most up-to-date audio visual equipment. Others can only provide tape-recorder, some have spare rooms in which interviews could be carried out, others hardly have enough space to implement the existing time-table . Action research must be designed in such a way as to be easily implemented within the pattern of constraints existing within the school.

Any initial definition of the research problem with almost certainly be modified as the research proceeds. Nevertheless, this definition is important because it helps to set limits to the enquiry. For example, a teacher sets out to explore thorugh action research the problems of how to start a lesson effectively. The research will tend to focus upon the first few minutes of the lesson. The question of what data to collect is very largely answered by a clear definition of the research problem. So, the researchers must need to define the problem clearly. Then, they can folloe the corrective or right direction to gather the useful or related data to carry one enquiring any questions concern the specific problem topic more resonable or rational.

In conclusion, the principal justification for the use of action research in the context of the school is improvement of practice. This can be achieved only if teachers are able to change their better attitudes and teaching behavior to be felt to students. So, if the researchers hope their researches can be implemented successfully. They need to know their action researchs are relied chiefly on how observation and behavioral data is gathered. If the school's researchers can observe sample teachers and students how and why the sample students' learning behaviors are influenced by their sample teachers' teaching method. Then, they can find the more accurate judgement hoe to improve teaching performance or raise their teaching efficiencies more easily.

reference

Plewis, I. " Pupils progress in reading and maths during primary school: association with ethnic group and sex.", Educational research, 33, (1991) , 133-40.